The Bitch Switch

Knowing How to Turn It On and Off

the Bitch Switch

Knowing How to Turn It On and Off

OMAROSA

Copyright © 2008 Omarosa Manigault-Stallworth & Phoenix Books, Inc.

ISBN-10: 1-59777-595-9
ISBN-13: 978-1-59777-595-3
Library of Congress Cataloging-In-Publication Data Available

Book Design by: Sonia Fiore

Printed in the United States of America

Phoenix Books, Inc.
9465 Wilshire Boulevard, Suite 840
Beverly Hills, CA 90212

10 9 8 7 6 5 4 3 2 1

To my mother,
THERESA MARIE MANIGAULT,

and in memory of my father,
JACK THOMAS MANIGAULT.

TABLE OF CONTENTS

INTRODUCTION

Why Women Need the
Bitch Switch

The genesis of this book began in the Old Executive Office Building of the White House during my appointment as Deputy Associate Director of Presidential Personnel.

At that time in my life I had certainly overextended myself. I was engaged to be married, going to school at night, teaching as an adjunct professor at the Graduate School, USDA on the weekends, and volunteering at the Maya Angelou Public Charter School. At work we were dealing with the possible impeachment of my boss, then-president Bill Clinton, and Al Gore's fund-raising scandal. At home I was busy planning a wedding for 400 guests, along with preparing lectures for class and term papers for my doctoral professors. It was organized chaos!

Since that time, I have been able to reflect on my unique journey. I have fought battles in the fields of politics, business, academia, and entertainment. In all of these arenas I noticed one thing: women are always in second place.

So what is the main culprit for this huge social disparity? We as women have allowed ourselves to be BULLIED by life! We whispered when we should have been shouting; we cried when we should have been clawing; we complained when we should have been campaigning; we complied when we should have been demanding. We asked "How high?" when we should have been saying "Hell NO!" We did not turn on our Bitch Switch to demand what we wanted, how we wanted it, and what the heck we were going to do once we got it.

This century has shown great progress for women, but also great losses. We are at an important crossroads in history. I was so inspired by Hillary Clinton's run for the presidential nomination, but the news coverage of her campaign was enough to discourage every young girl in this nation from ever even thinking of saying, "One day I want to be President." Hillary waited too late in the race to turn on her Bitch Switch, and it cost her the nomination. Martha Stewart's Bitch Switch got her put behind bars.

Carly Fiorina, probably the most powerful woman in corporate America, and one who appeared to have her Bitch Switch turned to its highest setting, was forced out of her position as chairman and CEO of Hewlett-Packard though she recently reappeared as a high-level advisor to John McCain.

What we as women have gone by in the past—the nice-girl game plan—is NOT working in the office, at home, or in life! In romantic relationships, we suffer because we hand over our power for love and turn off our Bitch Switch. In our relationships with friends and family, we are taken advantage of. In the office, we have been passed over and walked on because we refuse to embrace our inner bitch. WELL, NO MORE!

Does that mean we should all storm into the office tomorrow and start raising hell? YES! But not exactly in that way. It's time for a new paradigm for how we, as women, approach our goal of making it to the top!

This book is about POWER! It's simple: they have it, and you want it. Do you desire clout and respect in business and at home? Do you want to stop being shrinking violets and doormats? Do you want to learn how to be tough when necessary? Then you're going to need to find your switch! And fast!

As a woman, you are uniquely armed with one of the greatest communication devices anyone can have: a BITCH SWITCH, from here on out sometimes referred to as "bSwitch." (Can men have bSwitches? Yes, but that's another chapter in another book.) You don't have to act like a man to get respect in the workplace. You don't have to be a man to take charge! Once your bSwitch goes on, that does not mean your femininity goes off.

Are you tired of being a coward—living daily in a constant state of anxiety? Do your insecurities weigh on your ability to grow and advance? Do you want to be the star of your own life—to realize your dreams and succeed? Then you will have to confront your current pattern of accommodation and acquire the skills to turn the *switch* on.

What Would Omarosa Do?

You are probably saying to yourself, "There is no way that I can just walk into a situation and turn on my bSwitch just like that. I would not know what to say or do." My suggestion to you in that situation is to think of a strong woman whom you admire and respect. If you don't know one, find one whose style you admire. Study that person and how she deals with conflict and turmoil in her life. And if you can't find that person, don't worry. Just think, "WWOD?" Throughout this book, I answer many letters from women who are faced with the ultimate dilemma—When to Bitch and When Not to Bitch.

As I traveled the world lecturing, I noticed a need for tactics that could empower women to work, to communicate effectively, and to lead with confidence. This book is designed to provide practical, usable tips that can help working women gain confidence, respect, and success by changing their way of communication. When you employ the tools of the bSwitch, you will find that these are tools of change—tools that will build your confidence and give you the ability to say things that you never had the courage to say before.

The thinking isn't that we can turn a pussycat into a pit bull. No, but a cat can be taught when to hiss and use her claws, and when to purr and preen, and be just as aggressive as any breed of dog (i.e., our male counterparts).

This book is your step-by-step guide for locating your inner BITCH, personalizing your switch, and knowing when to turn it on and when to turn it off. It's not about being mean. It's about meaning what you SAY! Again, the bSwitch is about power—who has it and who does not. In this book you will learn how to control the bSwitch to shift the power and shed light on any situation!

Throughout, I'll talk about the various bSwitches that I have encountered. In fairness to these women, they probably did not know that their behavior was being evaluated and classified by me at the time. Nonetheless, there were bSwitches a-clickin' when I interacted, worked, or lived with these women, and I definitely took notes!

After all is said and done, I truly hope that you locate and use your very own bSwitch and transform your life. Remember, life's a bitch, and life's got lots of sisters!

Omarosa

W.W.O.D.

Dear Omarosa,
I've seen you singled out as a "bitch" on almost every episode of The Apprentice. *Actually, almost every time you're on TV. As someone who's used to defending that title, I wanted to ask for your advice.*

I'm a junior in a Los Angeles university, and two months ago I started an internship at a huge corporate film studio. Since you've been thrust into this film/TV world, I thought maybe you'd have some good insight into the business. My boss is a high-level female executive, but to put it kindly— she's a raging bitch! I thought maybe since I was a woman myself, this would change her attitude toward me. I was wrong. It seems she is a bitch with everyone she encounters on the job. Now, I haven't seen her outside of work—maybe this is a trait that she ONLY employs 9–5—but even if she was just ACTING like a bitch to get her job done, wouldn't that bleed over into her personal life? How can she be happy with herself? Is this what it is really going to take to make it in this business?

I'm from the Midwest, and to be honest, I'd rather follow a different career path than change who I am.

What should I do?

Thanks in advance,
Bitch-in-Training

Dear B.I.T.,
Use that bitch as a bSwitch model! Who cares if she's a bitch in her personal life—use her as an example of how to be in the office. Once you're at her level, you decide your own fate. Just because you garnered the coveted "Female Exec" position doesn't mean you have to be a bitch. But to get to that point is going to take hard work, a healthy dose of self-esteem, and bswitch tactics.

Listen: The Bitch Switch may sound like a strange concept, but you don't have to give up who you are to get where you want to be. Be conscious of when your switch is on and off, stay strong, and don't give up! There's no reason you can't go after the stars—and bitch along the way.

Good luck!
Omarosa

PART I

THE BITCH SWITCH
What It Is and What It Does

I get called a bitch frequently. But what I never get called is a pushover, a doormat, or a weakling.

—Omarosa

Bitch in the Making

"You've won this round...but the night is still young."
—Alexis Carrington, "Dynasty"

Nearly ten years ago, long before my name and face became instantly recognizable to millions of people all over the world from Donald Trump's boardroom, I was busily running around Washington, D.C., accomplishing my goals. At that point in time, I was working as a presidential appointee in the White House and earning my doctorate. My carefully laid plans turned upside down on September 11, 2003, when *The Apprentice* burst on the scene, and I became instantly infamous as the über-bitch. My whole life has changed since then, but what you may not know is that even ten years ago I was passionate about teaching other women the Bitch Switch concept. I was just using different words.

I taught a class called Communication Skills for Women for the Graduate School, USDA for four years. Most of the women in the class worked for the U.S. Government at various levels and ranged in age from late twenties to late fifties. Working for the government has extremely attractive benefits: regular hours, excellent health and retirement plans, plenty of vacation time, discounts for government workers, job security, special programs for buying cars and houses, not to mention that a typical government office job runs like clockwork. You show up and do your job, nothing more and nothing less than what you can accomplish in exactly eight hours. Then you go home at five on the dot and come back and do it again the next day. People in Washington call them GGJs—Good Government Jobs—and once they secure one, most people stay until they retire, that is to say, for life. But what I discovered was that most of the women in my class wanted much more out of life.

I took instructing this class very seriously because I knew that it could change their lives! I asked each and every woman in the class to take a good hard look at herself and reevaluate. It was somewhat of a shock when I realized, quite young, that everybody was not like me. Most of my frustrations in my twenties arose from my desire to get the people around me to be as driven and hard-charging and goal-oriented as I was. I could not understand why people weren't as passionate about their own plans and goals and lives as I was about mine. **I wanted these women to understand the connection between passion and power!**

"Plan your work and work your plan!"
—Kevin L. Jefferson

BITCH SWITCH EXERCISE
on Long- and Short-Term GOALS

On the next page, make a list of your goals:
- Short-term (as in the next thirty days),
- Long-term (as in the next five years), and
- Lifelong (as in before you die).

This list will serve as the essential road map for your success!

Short-term

Long-term

Lifelong

"Good Enough" Isn't Good Enough!

As women we do just enough to get by. We get quite complacent and accepting of our lives, thinking that it's just enough to do all right at our jobs and be casual about our lives. This kind of thinking was incomprehensible to me. Why do just enough to get by when there's the death of you ahead? We only live once! That "good enough" attitude will just keep women doing what they've always done, and **when you keep doing what you've always done, you'll keep getting what you've always got.** For plenty of women, certainly many in my classes, they need a new plan.

It was true then and just as true now: When I take a good look at the state of working women around me, it saddens me that so many of them have been browbeaten, undermined, groped, backstabbed and patronized along the way. So many women—and I mean women all over America, in every kind of job, at every level—have just had it. They are sick and tired of being sick and tired, in second place, and invisible!

My syllabus promised to teach women not only the necessary skills to communicate with authority and impact but also how to incorporate these skills into their daily work lives. It would also assist women with their personal goals and career advancement. I firmly believed then, as I do now, that changing her attitude, outlook, and communication style can turn a woman's life around, rejuvenate her career and romantic life, and help her attain what she's been seeking all along.

As you work through this part of the book, you will come across a series of exercises meant to help you discover your very own bSwitch. Maybe it's never surfaced before—but it's there! Use the space provided to jot down your thoughts, goals, and dreams, and soon enough, you'll find your inner power...and BITCH SWITCH!

R-E-S-P-E-C-T

"If particular care and attention is not paid to the ladies, we are determined to foment a rebellion, and will not hold ourselves bound by any laws in which we have no voice or representation." -Abigail Adams

A major component of the bSwitch is respect. I believe that it is crucial for every woman to speak and act in a manner that compels others to respect her. In my case, people may not have always liked me or my unorthodox tactics, but they always respected my work. I may not have been likable, but I was sensible and kept the end goal in mind. I was respected because I got the job done. Yes, I did it in my own way—edgy—but things got done and the task was accomplished. That's what a leader does!

Too many times women change the essence of who they are to match the expectations of what they hope to get back from a boss, a partner, the world. I didn't teach that class or write this book to try to change a woman's nature, but merely show her the power of a tool she already has inside, just waiting to be turned on! The message is the same as it was back when I was trying to motivate women to empower themselves; only the words have changed.

Now I call it the **Bitch Switch.**

Who Are the Killjoys?

Learning when to turn the bSwitch on and turn it off begins with identifying the killjoys in your life.

It almost goes without saying, but you must first properly identify them so you can devise a plan of action to effectively deal with those who sap your energy and well-being. It's also important to understand their motivation: are they intentionally trying to make your life miserable, or are they just miserable people who have no joy in their own lives and don't want you to have any either?

So, who exactly are the killjoys? Can you recognize them or are they wolves in sheep's clothing?

As their title might suggest, the killjoys are the social ticks who eat away at you every day—they might be supervisors, coworkers, clients, even family members and boyfriends. Their bites may be small and undetected, but will destroy you over time. They can shatter your self-confidence with one curt statement and chip away at your self-esteem by being demeaning and condescending. Killjoys de-motivate you and sap you of all your energy. Their toxicity is palpable, hindering your ability to accomplish simple tasks and focus on your ultimate happiness. They are abrasive and abusive and the mere sound of their voices can make you feel ill. Killjoys rob you of the HOPE that things can, and will, get better. They make you feel worthless and erase what little morale you have built up over the years. Killjoys encourage dissension and thrive in an environment where chaos and mistrust reign.

Don't waste your time trying to *change* killjoys—the bSwitch gives you a guide to effectively *deal* with them. I promise you, killjoys are no match against the power of the bSwitch...really! You will never be able to change who they are, but you can change the way killjoys respond to you and treat you. I firmly

believe that we TEACH PEOPLE HOW THEY
SHOULD TREAT US!

....

Change Your Actions, Not Your Nature

"I myself have never been able to find out precisely what
feminism is; I only know that people call me a feminist
whenever I express sentiments that differentiate me from
a doormat." —Rebecca West

Let's start with a disclaimer. Being tough
tends to be embedded in the DNA. Most tough
women are born; some are made, but it's much
easier when you're born that way! However, I do
believe that every woman can be coached to rise
to the occasion when necessary—activate her
bSwitch—then return to her natural comfort level.

Below is an exercise I always found very
helpful in my classes. This quiz will highlight
personality traits so you will be able to see where
you are on the Bitch Switch scale. From there,
you can easily see how much work you'll need to
do to flip on your bSwitch! Most women need a
lot of help, some are appropriately assertive, and
a very few need to tone it down a little. But there
are ways to effectively communicate no matter
what type you are, which we will discuss later in
this book.

What Is Your Normal Behavior Style?

Circle all the words below that you think describe your behavior at work. Then ask a coworker to circle the traits that he or she believes apply to you. See if your coworker's perception of you matches your own. Add or remove circles until you're satisfied that the most accurate words to describe YOU are circled.

Critical	Industrious	Pushy	Strong-willed
Indecisive	Persistent	Severe	Independent
Stuffy	Serious	Tough	Practical
Picky	Expecting	Dominating	Decisive
Moralistic	Orderly	Harsh	Efficient
Aloof	Thoughtful	Cold	Goal-oriented
Conforming	Supportive	Manipulative	Ambitious
Unsure	Respectful	Excitable	Stimulating
Ingratiating	Willing	Undisciplined	Enthusiastic
Dependent	Dependable	Reactive	Dramatic
Awkward	Agreeable	Egotistical	Friendly
Wishy-washy	Approachable	Flaky	Creative

Draw two straight lines down and across to divide the word list into four equal rectangles (one down the center top-to-bottom and one side-to-side). In which quarter are the most words circled? Compare this with the model below to determine your primary and secondary styles.

SMART BITCH!

Who she is: Works with existing circumstances to promote quality in products and services.

TOUGH BITCH!

Who she is: Shapes the environment by overcoming opposition in order to get immediate results.

PLEASER!

Who she is: Cooperates with others, makes sure people are included, and feels good about the process.

PUSHOVER!

Who she is: Shapes the environment by bringing others into an alliance to generate enthusiasm for results.

This exercise will help you establish your baseline. You'll recognize that there are different ways to communicate with each of these various types of switches. The idea when I taught this exercise in my class was to always be strong and assertive, whether or not it was your natural style. Sadly, for most women, it was very far from their true nature.

W.W.O.D.

Hi,
I'm going to be quite honest. All the so-called "most powerful" women in this country not only seem like power-hungry bitches, but they come across as downright egomaniacal! Is this really the example I want my young daughter to follow? Oprah, Martha, Hillary, and even you, Omarosa—the one thing all of you have in common is your big, fat EGO. So if not you, who can my daughter—and the rest of her generation—look up to?

—Call Me Old-Fashioned, Orlando, FL

Dear Oldy,
I take it as a true compliment to be included in such an extraordinary group of women. Do the most powerful MEN in the world—with their equally inflated egos—trigger such disgust? Your double standard for your own sex IS old-fashioned. The fact that we can even have a discussion about "powerful" women and the meaning of the word "bitch" is a sign that women have progressed in society. Despite your outdated views of how women should and should not be, I wouldn't be surprised if your very own daughter is president of the United States or topping the Forbes 100 one day soon—thanks to the "egomaniacs" before her, of course.

Good luck to you!
Omarosa

Using What You Have to Get What You Want

*"If you want something said, ask a man;
if you want something done, ask a woman."*
–Margaret Thatcher

The bSwitch is all about doing whatever it takes to advance your goals, and that isn't always about being rude and aggressive. There's an old saying about getting more bees with honey than vinegar. (But honey, don't forget—bees sting!) Let's not discard the power of charm and friendliness, neither of which would seem to have much to do with the bSwitch. They are, however, powerful weapons that I frequently employ—because flipping the switch takes energy, and why not save it for when you truly need it? There are other tactics to try first. Finding common ground and charming people top the list.

There are numerous examples of when my charm has helped me get what I want without lifting a finger to flip my switch. A fashion designer whose sportswear I love—everyone in Hollywood does—has a notoriously uncooperative gatekeeper who controls his appointments. This woman is really tough—believe me, I know a bitch when I see one! She's uncooperative, cranky, and she makes it nearly impossible to get an appointment. She couldn't care less who you are.

I have learned to handle her in the best way for this particular situation: Always keeping in mind what I want...those fabulous designer clothes! I took the time to learn a few things about her, and now whenever I go in I ask, "How's your son doing in soccer? Oh, by the way, here is an article about gardening that I thought you might like." Hey, it's no sweat for me to clip the article, and I happen to know that this woman's passions are gardening and, of course, her son. Now the two of us get along just fine, although I see and hear her on the phone biting every other client's head off.

In this particular case, the very first time I encountered this woman I realized I was dealing with someone who already had her bSwitch going on FULL POWER, twenty-four hours a day. It would be a very volatile situation—a major electrical storm—if I had mine turned on too! (Not that I couldn't, mind you, but it's all about using the switch judiciously.) Engaging in a battle with this woman would slow me down from my objective, so I found a way to get her to turn it down a notch! Trouble averted, objective reached! bSwitch deactivated!

Use the Switch Wisely!

"She's the kind of girl who climbed the ladder of success wrong by wrong." –Mae West

We can't all be running around wreaking havoc all the time—it would be a world full of BBBs (Bitches Behaving Badly)! And trust me, that's the last thing I'm advocating. The Bitch Switch is never an excuse to be pissy without provocation!

From Zero to Bitch in 2.5 Seconds

"I'm not afraid of storms, for I'm learning to sail my ship." –Louisa May Alcott

It's imperative that you are always ready, willing, and able to access your switch in any given situation. I make it a rule to be friendly with the executive assistants of powerful people, however; they can be an invaluable source of information and assistance to you when dealing with their bosses. One of my top clients had a lovely woman as his assistant, and we grew quite friendly over the months. She was very efficient and good at her job, but I liked her personally as well. Unfortunately, she eventually grew quite casual about our relationship, because the line between professional and personal became blurred.

I started noticing that my company invoices were being paid later and later each month. One month, the check never arrived, so

I called her and spoke to her twice about it. Both times she said, "Oh, we're just so backed up here—tomorrow for sure. You know how it is." Yes, I know how it is, and I let it slide. But the third time it happened, I had had enough. I am in business to make money, and I take my business—and my money—very seriously. I drove over to the office and confronted her: "What is going on here? I have asked you three times for this payment. It was due a week ago. I am sitting here until that check is cut—I'm not leaving this office until it's in my hand."

My bSwitch was on, and she was really surprised, and a bit afraid, because she had never seen that side of me before. There was no reason she ever would have had to. In the end, I took half the responsibility for this situation because I had allowed her to think that it was all right for her to put my stuff on the back burner. Now I was making it clear that it wasn't all right.

Miraculously, this elusive check was somehow cut and signed in fifteen minutes. For the first time in a long time, as I sat waiting for the check, she offered me coffee. We had become too friendly for the regular business niceties. I realized, as she kept anxiously asking me if I needed anything, that I had taught her to treat me as though my business and needs were unimportant. It was a very good lesson. We never returned to our former level of friendliness; she returned to being cordial, treating me like any other business partner. I, in turn, treated her politely but professionally. I was relieved. Charm and friendliness are effective, but you must never let them get in the way of business! When they do, it's time for the switch!

The Switch Goes On

"Don't compromise yourself. You are all you've got."
—Janice Joplin

By far, the first and hardest hurdle for women to overcome in changing their communication style and flipping on the bSwitch is the universal need to be liked. There was even a time when this was difficult for me. No doubt I always had an edge—that's just in my genes—but I grew up in Ohio, the heartland, where it was nice to be important, but more important to be nice. And I was still living very much by that ideal. I quickly discovered that my niceness was a hindrance in the cutthroat political arena of Washington, D.C. As a good girl, I was laughed at and looked down upon, which came as quite a shock.

My first major bSwitch moment was during my first month in the Office of Presidential Personnel at the White House. I reported directly to a woman we shall call Ann, the head of our department. This woman was a wolf in sheep's clothing. She pretended to be supportive and excited about my working for her, but she constantly sabotaged my efforts.

My best friend from college, Shannon, was visiting from Ohio, a trip we'd planned for months and that I was very excited about. I was anxious to wrap up the workweek and show Shannon around town. Late that Friday afternoon, Ann told me that our offices were being painted that weekend, and that I was going to have to come in both days to supervise. She didn't want to waste her days off coming in and letting painters in and out.

"You need to stay late tonight and then be here in the morning by eight to let them in. Make sure to stick around and keep an eye on them. OK," she said, gathering her bags and standing at the door, "I'm leaving." My girlfriend was just sitting there beside me, ready to tour the West Wing, watching our plans disappear into thin air.

For the first time, I went from zero to BITCH in 2.5 seconds. "You can leave, but I'm leaving too," I told my boss. "I can't come in until Monday. I have plans this weekend and can't work." My friend's mouth fell open. Even I was surprised at the words that had come out of my mouth. I had just gotten a really good job, and I loved working in the White House. I suppose I could have been fired for this response. But what was important to me in that moment was taking care of myself and standing up for *me*. I had a choice: I could be a doormat and let my boss walk all over me, or I could stand up for myself. Something happened in that moment—the bSwitch went on.

The reaction was immediate. Ann looked at me, surprised, not sure how to respond for a moment. She then said, "You know, I do remember you saying that you had things you had to do this weekend. Maybe I can call somebody to open up the offices tomorrow and Sunday." She backed down immediately. Shannon sat there amazed; she still talks about that moment to this day.

I will never stop being an Ohio girl and everything that comes with that until the day I die. In civilized society we need to have social niceties and politeness. In shark-infested environments like the District and Hollywood, many people, particularly men, take a highly arrogant, abrasive approach to business that I don't like, because part of me will always be that girl from the Midwest, being polite, saying and constantly watching out for people's feelings. It was hard to realize that, yes, I was absolutely going to have to flip that bSwitch on if I wanted to survive. But I did it and never looked back.

"**B**(abe) **I**(n)
T(otal) **C**(ontrol)
of **H**(erself)"

The Bitch Not to Be Messed With!

"Only good girls keep diaries. Bad girls don't have time."
-Tallulah Bankhead

Years later, on my application for *The Apprentice,* one of the questions was: "How would your coworkers describe you?" My response: "As a bitch, not to be messed with!" I was very aware of what others thought of me, but that never slowed me down from what I wanted to accomplish.

More likely than not, if you are focused and driven and don't allow other people's drama to derail your own success, then you are probably going to be called a bitch. You might be the most successful, but not the best-liked. The Bitch Switch is not about making friends or destroying friendships. It's about being a friend to yourself and not allowing others to take advantage of you or your friendship!

If you're looking for a book about making friends, then I suggest Dale Carnegie's classic, *How to Win Friends & Influence People.* It's a great book that teaches you how to get people to like you. Likability is important, but just because you use the power of the bSwitch does not mean that you won't be liked.

The power of the switch is about what you stand for and what you won't stand for! A woman in control of her switch determines her own rules of engagement for every situation. She establishes them with a look, her demeanor, and her delivery. She has the POWER to control her own destiny!

When you stop caring about what people think about you, you tap into your own creative freedom. YOU define for yourself who you are, what you are, and what you stand for! You also have options! You can choose to deal with a certain person or not! If a person is toxic and you no longer want him or her in your life, flip the bSwitch on and you will have the courage to remove that person!

Turning on the bSwitch is nothing more than changing your attitude—your voice, your gestures, and your facial expressions. It's an energy change, and you can easily feel its power when it's on. It's a very effective tool, and mastering it will make every aspect of your life much easier.

Isn't that why you're reading this book?

Switch On, Switch Off!

There was a commercial that ran in the nineties advertising a gizmo called "The Clapper." The idea was, all you had to do was clap your hands to turn the lights or the television on and off. Some women have so much power and control over their switch that it's as easy as a clap of the hands to use when necessary.

The perfect example of this type of woman is, of course, **Oprah Winfrey.** She holds so much power in the palm of her hand that she rarely has to flip that switch on. The great thing about her is that when anybody picks a fight with her, she fights back fiercely. She does not back down when anybody tries to tarnish her reputation or image. She doesn't hesitate to flip the switch!

I remember years ago during her legal battle with the Cattlemen's Association, she appeared visibly upset while going in and out of court. I remember watching that entire posse of men in Texas, all in their cowboy hats, gathered against her. Oprah armed herself with a great team, which included Dr. Phil McGraw, and fought back with the boldness and aggressiveness that all women should know how to display!

She flipped that switch on when she needed to, and defeated those cattle ranchers. More recently, her switch was on full power when she called out James Frey, whose memoir she had chosen for her book club and which turned out to be completely fabricated.

I applaud Oprah for being the Clapper, the supreme example of how women should use their own bSwitch!

Bitch Switch Tips!

- There is an intrinsic connection between passion and power!
- If you keep doing what you've always done, you will get what you've always got!
- Plan your work and work your plan!
- The Bitch Switch is about POWER and RESPECT!

PART II

Locating Your SWITCH

"I'm tough, ambitious, and know exactly what I want. If that makes me a bitch, okay."
–Madonna

Stop Worrying About What Others Think of You

"Nothing makes a woman more beautiful than the belief that she is beautiful." -Sophia Loren

As a teen I was indoctrinated in the whole self-esteem and women's empowerment movement. Educators encouraged young girls like me to use such phrases as "I like myself!" and "I'm great!" Plenty of girls said the words, but for many their meaning never resonated deep inside. With the power of the bSwitch you will think it, mean it, and live it! Because you truly have the power to be the greatest force in your life.

When I was teaching my communications class for women, I identified the single most debilitating habit women practiced: worrying about what others thought, whether people liked or accepted them. During class I challenged women to speak openly about their goals and dreams. Most of those dreams and aspirations were never realized due to the fear of what others would think. They would say, "Professor, I can't do that. What would people say?" or, "If I fail, what will people think of me?" As a result, many of my students put a limit on their life's potential and placed themselves in a self-imposed prison.

BITCH SWITCH EXERCISE

What would you attempt if
you knew you absolutely could not fail?
Detail in the space provided.

I have guided many students through this dark reality that faces many of us. Most of them lived daily in the shadow of someone else's opinion. I encouraged them—and I encourage YOU—not to hold onto the fear of what others might think.

It is a terrible habit that must be broken! The women in my class were paralyzed by the fear of failure. But I urged them, and I urge you, to live your life as if other people's opinions don't matter. BECAUSE THEY DON'T. The only opinion that counts is your own. This is not a shallow pep talk; it is the foundation of the power of the bSwitch! The sky is the limit when you stop worrying about the opinion of someone you know or love, much less someone you don't even know!

BITCH SWITCH EXERCISE
Who do you listen to?

I always taught my students to give the most consideration, outside of themselves, to what I call the three F's of influence: Friends, Family, and those affecting your Financial stability. In the diagram on the next page, fill in the names of those people who make up the three F's in YOUR life.

Three F's of Influence

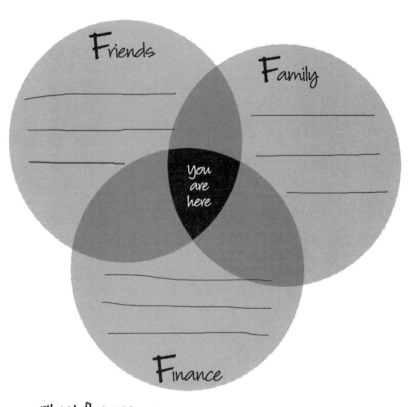

Other Influences

_____

_____

_____

_____

_____

It's my theory that you would not spend so much time on the opinions of others if you knew what little time and effort others really spent thinking about your success and failure.

The best way to overcome this bad habit is to replace it with a positive one. Start by making a list of all the good and positive qualities that you have. I am certain that as the list grows, so will your confidence. Once you convince yourself that you have it going on, others will see it too!

W.W.O.D.

Omarosa,
I was always quite shy in school—I never looked people eye-to-eye, I kept my bangs long and in my face, and I dreaded school functions. At one point during my senior year, I heard that the boy I had a crush on liked me (gasp!) but thought I was too "mean"! I was completely shocked. I could hardly speak when he passed by, and here he was calling me "mean"?

How could I be making such an awful impression on people?

Sincerely,
Nice Girl (I promise!)

Dear Nicey,
If I ever saw a case of low self-esteem, this is it. Long hair hanging in your face, shuffling in the hall, trying to blend in to the background—girl, you needed a makeover. And not just a haircut and brighter wardrobe, but an INTERNAL makeover. You needed to realize what's great about you! You already knew the boy you'd been crushing on liked you—and there were others, too. Look deep down inside of yourself and find out why. Once you're confident and happy with yourself, you will unconsciously project that image on those around you. You can't use the power of the Bitch Switch when you don't know and love yourself—inside and out.

Good luck!
Omarosa

The Big Squeeze

For many years I served as an international pageant trainer. I successfully trained contestants from the countries of Guyana, Taiwan, and the United States. I always looked for fun analogies to get the contestants to stay motivated to win.

One of my favorite analogies that I used when I was serving as pageant trainer to then-Miss District of Columbia Teen USA, who was training for the Miss Teen USA pageant, was THE BIG SQUEEZE.

The essence of who and what you are needs to be strong and consistent all the way to your very core. You might normally be a very lovely, calm person. But under pressure, you don't know what's going to come out! You must work on what's inside, so that when you're being squeezed, the right reaction comes out!

Think about a peach: Lovely and soft on the outside, and no matter how hard you squeeze it, the only thing that comes out is sweet, delicious peach juice. That is the essence of the peach. You certainly don't want to be an onion, which is perfectly fine when it's just sitting there harmless, but when it gets squeezed, all that comes out is smelly liquid that makes people cry—and burns, too!

Learning to use your bSwitch is all about grace under pressure.

By the way, I consider myself to be a kiwi! Exotic taste and not easy to get!

From Pitiful to Powerful-It Starts With Forgiveness.

"I don't know if I continue, even today, always liking myself. But what I learned to do many years ago was to forgive myself. It is very important for every human being to be able to forgive herself or himself because if you live, you will make mistakes-it is inevitable. But once you do and you see the mistake, then you forgive yourself and say, 'well, if I'd known better, I'd have done better,' that's all.... If we all hold on to the mistake, we can't see our own glory in the mirror because we have the mistake between our faces and the mirror; we can't see what we've capable of being. You can ask forgiveness of others, but in the end the real forgiveness is in one's own self. I think that young men and women are so caught by the way they see themselves. Now mind you. When a larger society sees them as unattractive, as threats, as too black or too white or too poor or too fat or too thin or too sexual or too asexual, that's rough. But you can overcome that. The real difficulty is to overcome how you think about yourself. If we don't have that we never grow, we never learn, and sure as hell we should never teach." -Maya Angelou

Like Who You Are–If You Don't, I Won't!

"A strong, positive self-image is the best possible preparation for success." –Joyce Brothers

Here's a tough one for many women to grasp: ***Your identity does not have to be tied to pleasing people.*** You can please or displease anyone, and it doesn't change the essence of who you are. Too many times women tie their identity to their ability to make others happy. If I don't make my boss or my friends happy at every moment, does that make me a bad or less valuable person? If I do make them happy, does that make me a better person? No, it only means that on this particular occasion you were able to give them what they wanted or needed—nothing more, nothing less! Remember, you can't please all people all the time. Disappointing folks is a part of life and should not alter how you feel about yourself!

I felt that way about boys when I was growing up, and men now. If a man doesn't like me, the problem lies with him, not with me. I don't internalize his dislikes as my personal shortcoming. I never question if I am sexy enough for him or nice enough. I never alter the essence of who I am in order to win affection. I don't compromise myself by trying to be all things to all people.

There are some very good books for women about letting go of these "pleaser" traits if this is your trouble area. My favorite, one that I recommend to all young women just starting out in business, is Kate White's wonderful *Why Good Girls Don't Get Ahead But Gutsy Girls Do*. When I read her book as a young executive, it was as if a light went on—it was the first time I realized I was not alone in how I felt about my approach to business and life!

When I lecture at high schools, I encourage the teenage girls not to lose themselves in their attempts to be the funny girl in the class, or a promiscuous girl to get boys to pay attention to her, or a constant giver, the girl who buys things for all her friends and does whatever the group asks of her to be accepted. I help them to see that they are just setting themselves up to be taken advantage of.

It's important to surround yourself with people who bring out the best in you. The key is to find those who create an environment that is conducive for growth and success. Find people in your life who will tell you like it TRULY is. I have close girlfriends (Shannon, Kim, Wendy, Malesa, Renee, Huda, and Damola) who always help me stay grounded and REAL.

I realize that without these strong female relationships women can become susceptible to very bad advice from mass media. Women's magazines tell you that if you diet and wear designer labels then your life will be complete. Television commercials feature models and actresses who push products that promise perfection in a bottle. The greatest asset that you can have is a team of people who will make sure that you are on track to reach your full potential. Use your bSwitch to weed out those killjoys who are disguised as friends.

How Do You Speak to Yourself?

"I got my start by giving myself a start."
—Theresa Manigault, aka Momarosa

Everyone has an inner voice; a personal critic. Far too many women have a harsh, scolding voice in their heads that constantly uses words that limit them, such as "stupid" or "fat." Practice saying positive things about yourself. Building your self-esteem must become a habit. Do not beat yourself up for what could have been. Just remember a rhyme from my mom (also known as Momarosa): good, better, best, never let it rest—till your good is your better, and your better is your best.

WHAT WOULD MOMAROSA DO?

"The road to success is not straight. There is a curve called Failure, a loop called Confusion, speed bumps called Friends, red lights called Enemies, caution lights called Family. You will have flats called Jobs. But, if you have a spare called Determination, an engine called Perseverance, insurance called Faith, and a driver called Jesus, you will make it to a place called Success."   —Momarosa

"Recipe for success: Study while others are sleeping; work while others are loafing; prepare while others are playing; and dream while others are wishing."
                                                            —William A. Ward

"Find something you love, and find a way to make an honest living out of it."   —Momarosa

"A journey of a thousand miles begins with a single step."   —Confucius

"Choose a job you love, and you will never have to work a day in your life."   —Confucius

"I do not want a friend who smiles when I smile, who weeps when I weep, for my shadow in the pool can do better than that." *—Confucius*

"There is no royal flower-strewn path to success. And if there is, I have not found it, for if I have accomplished anything in life it is because I have been willing to work hard." *—Madam C. J. Walker*

Allow Your Passion to Propel You

"Just don't give up trying to do what you really want to do. Where there is love and inspiration, I don't think you can go wrong." -Ella Fitzgerald

The best advice I can give about feeling good about yourself is to reflect upon your passion in life. Even if you have to look all the way back to your childhood to remember doing something you loved, something that made you happy and excited and that you felt good about—that's the feeling you should be looking to recapture in your life now! What were those dreams? Believe it or not, when I was younger I wanted to be a weather girl. I loved the challenge that came with trying to predict the unpredictable. At the time, I was passionate about my dream of issuing storm alerts and standing in front of that funny weather map. Of course after a couple of close calls with tornado storms in my native Ohio, I shifted my focus to legal and business communications. But I never let go of the creative passion that set me on that path.

BITCH SWITCH EXERCISE
GOALS

Truthfully answer—as best as you can remember, what were your earliest career goals? Was it to become the first female president or to be the CEO of a Fortune 500 company? Reflect and list your earliest dreams here.

_____

_____

_____

_____

_____

_____

_____

_____

_____

_____

_____

_____

_____

_____

When you're fully engaged and passionate about doing things that you love, your insecurities and self-esteem problems will dwindle—you'll be too busy to dwell on negative feelings! Don't allow other people's drama to distract you from your own personal mission. Be selfish with your dreams and your time. You will never accomplish your goals if all your time is spent putting others before yourself. Use the bSwitch to make your dreams a priority!

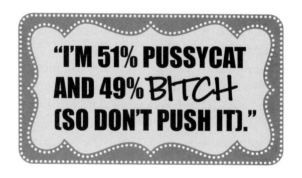

"I'M 51% PUSSYCAT AND 49% BITCH (SO DON'T PUSH IT)."

Life: Your Own Personal Reality Show

"Life is what we make it, always has been, always will be." – Grandma Moses

I have appeared on some of the most outrageous reality shows on TV: *The Surreal*

Life, Celebrity Fear Factor, and *Girls Behaving Badly.* While participating in these shows I did things I never imagined that I could do. On *Fear Factor* I traversed a rope that was held up fifty feet in the air by two helicopters. On *The Surreal Life,* I took motocross training with stuntman Carey Hart, and on *Girls Behaving Badly,* I posed as a naughty nurse in order to "punk" an innocent patient in a medical office.

While these shows were quite entertaining, they did little to reflect real life scenarios. (Seriously, would you ever stick your arm in a box of African tree boa snakes as I did on *Fear Factor?*) These scenarios *are* extreme and are an excellent way to escape the monotony of day-to-day life. But they do little to give us a dose of what's real and what's not in our own personal situations. Too often, women completely check out of their own lives. They escape into reality shows, soap operas, or romance novels and disappear into a fantasy life of some sort. Use the bSwitch to return to your own reality. What's going on in your real life? I'm sure it's quite interesting if you are fully engaged and involved in what's happening—that is, as long as you've set some goals and are actively working toward them.

You need to fully tap into your own situation. You are the only person who can control your destiny; you are the only person who can rejuvenate your own life. You cannot base decisions on other people's ability to provide you with joy or satisfaction, for you will always be disappointed. ***You can't look to anybody to provide you with something that isn't already inside!***

BITCH SWITCH EXERCISE

SELF-ANALYSIS

Take a moment to ask yourself the following questions:

- Do you express your needs and feelings to the people you love?
- Do you allow friends to take advantage of you?
- Do you stand up for what you believe in—to anyone, anywhere?
- Do you allow your anger to boil inside, eventually bursting for the wrong reasons?
- Do people walk all over you to get what they want?
- Is shyness preventing you from ever flipping on the Bitch Switch?

If you answered *yes* to any of the above, then you're in dire need of the power of the BITCH SWITCH. Keep reading for tips on how to improve your personal communication skills.

The Mechanics of the Switch

"You take your life in your own hands, and what happens? A terrible thing: no one to blame." —Erica Jong

Self-esteem fluctuates every day (hell, every minute of every hour). It's how you respond to these fluctuations that is going to be key in effectively utilizing your Bitch Switch. The true mechanics of the bSwitch are based on building a solid sense of confidence, self-esteem, and inner power. But what I've seen is one misconception over and over again: That self-esteem is a place you go, a destination you arrive at someday after you've done enough work on yourself, inside and out. Once you attain that elusive high self-esteem, you think, you will have arrived, and only then will life begin. Not only that, but it'll be a cakewalk from that point on.

WRONG! Self-esteem is a day-to-day battle with both your conscious and subconscious mind. Essentially, it's what value you place upon yourself. One minute you might feel great about yourself; the next you think—*momentarily*—"Oh my gawd, I am a complete mess!" The bSwitch is about regulating these fluctuations.

From Can't-Do to Can-Do!

"When one door of happiness closes, another opens; but often we look so long at the closed door that we do not see the one which has opened for us." -Helen Keller

What if you feel that you are simply not wired for a Bitch Switch? That you don't have the power or the energy required? I guarantee that the flicker is there, and you can find it. Maybe your power source is just a tiny little lightning bug right now, barely winking on, but I know it's there.

The reason I know it's there is because you picked up this book! Whether you bought it, borrowed it, or are just leafing through it, you have a desire to improve your condition. You're tired of being walked on. You're tired of people taking advantage of you. You're tired of being pushed around and passed over. The glimmer is there...this is all about illuminating it.

It's much easier to beat yourself up and let negative thoughts take over than it is to tell yourself how great you are. It's easy to give up and say, "The world hates me and I hate myself too," and sit around feeling sorry for yourself. That's what doormats are accustomed to doing. It is much more difficult to look at the world from a positive, optimistic viewpoint. It is going to take more than just desire in order to locate your bSwitch. It will require behavior modification and a completely new outlook on life in order for change to occur. Commit to shifting your attitude from can't-do to can-do!

BITCH SWITCH EXERCISE

One of the most important parts of finding, developing, and using your bSwitch is keeping the motor running! To remind yourself what you CAN DO—what you are truly capable of—use the blank spaces below to make a list of your past accomplishments. Impressive, right?

_____

_____

_____

_____

_____

_____

_____

_____

_____

What Powers the bSwitch?

"It's better to be a lion for a day than a sheep all your life." -Sister Elizabeth Kenny

When your self-esteem is low, or you find yourself thinking negative and self-sabotaging thoughts, that's the time to turn on the bSwitch. You may find you have to summon more of its power to get through a particularly tough or trying day. You may wonder, Where does the  power of the Bitch Switch come from? It must come from a profound internal drive to be the best you can be. Picture an old electric generator: sometimes it's just humming quietly along, sometimes it's blasting and clanking, and sometimes it's broken and you have to kick it a few times to get it working again.

Power is accumulated and stored in this generator by accomplishing personal daily goals or big long-term goals. The concept is similar to solar power—when the sun shines all day, all kinds of appliances can run off that stored energy later. Savor your accomplishments and triumphs—the small ones and the big ones—and keep the positive energy you accumulate in this generator. When you have a big stressful day ahead, you know there's plenty of stored energy to draw upon if and when you need to flip on the bSwitch.

To assemble your switch there must be some self-reflections. The wiring of your switch will be derived from your personal outlook, experiences, training, and unique point of view. It's important to begin with baby steps. I'm not talking about running out and confronting the entire world. I am talking little steps, like confronting the clerk at your local 7-Eleven who is rude to you every single day when you stop in for your coffee or newspaper. The next time he slaps your change on the counter and shoves your newspaper at you, look at him and say, "Your behavior is unacceptable. I'm sure you'll get it together by tomorrow morning." Baby steps!

Your spouse, for example, who may find it comical to address you by a derogatory pet name. Or co-worker who constantly mispronounces your name. Next time someone says, "Hey, Julia," reply authoritatively, "My name is Julie, Mr. Hooked-on-Phonics!" Baby steps!

The Bitch Switch is about powering up every aspect of your life! If you can get through this tough day, one situation at a time, you can get through tomorrow. If you can get through tomorrow, you can make it through next week. If you can make it through the week, you will get through this year. Each step of the way, you meet small goals—though I'm all about big goals, the bigger the better. But many tiny goals add up to big ones!

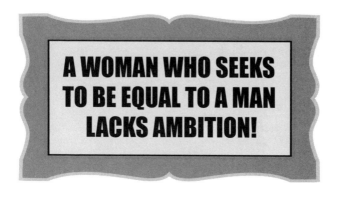

A WOMAN WHO SEEKS TO BE EQUAL TO A MAN LACKS AMBITION!

W.W.O.D.

Omarosa,
I desperately need your help! I told my soon-to-be sister-in-law that I would sing a song for her and my brother at their upcoming rehearsal dinner. I've been told I have a good voice, although I've never sung professionally, and I'm beyond nervous. Just thinking about standing up there on stage is making me break out in a sweat. I feel like it's too late to say "No" now.

Do you ever get nervous in front of crowds? Do you have any tricks or secrets you can let me in on? Any tips will be GREATLY appreciated (by me, my sister-in-law, and her entire wedding party)!

Thank you thank you thank you,
Scared Silent

Dear Scared,
As I've detailed in my book, I was born with guts. Luckily I never felt afraid on stage or in front of large groups of people; that always came naturally to me. But I understand not all women have these same genes. To help you overcome your stage fright, make sure you turn on your Bitch Switch before you even enter the room. Remind yourself (as many times as it takes!) how AWESOME you are and what a great HONOR you've been given. After all, your brother's soon-to-be wife asked you to prepare a song for a reason. And as soon as you hear the sound of applause filling the room, you'll be quick to remember the power of the switch next time, too!

Good luck!
Omarosa

The Switch Requires Focus

"I know God will not give me anything I can't handle.
I just wish that He didn't trust me so much."
-Mother Theresa

Turning on the bSwitch requires a great deal of discipline and focus. Focus is a skill that can be practiced and perfected. I've learned to do it, and with the bSwitch so can you!

You can't be a bad-ass on Tuesday and go back to being a doormat on Friday; you have to commit to learning how to manage your bSwitch. Being consistently focused on the task at hand is the only way you're going to be effective! Remember: **When you flip on the bSwitch, you'd better have something to say.** It has to pack a punch. And that all goes back to hard mental focus and preparedness. Once you put in the hard work and commitment, it's only then that you can start using your Bitch Switch to take you to the next level.

BITCH SWITCH QUIZ
WHERE ARE YOU ON THE BITCH SWITCH SCALE?

Some women are like doormats—they've never turned their switch ON. Others are too aggressive and desperately need to turn their switch DOWN. Take the following quiz and see where you fit on the BITCH SWITCH SCALE!

1. I enjoy receiving compliments.
○ Strongly disagree
○ Disagree
○ Agree
○ Strongly agree

2. I have a hard time giving criticism.
○ Strongly disagree
○ Disagree
○ Agree
○ Strongly agree

3. I feel uncomfortable asking for a raise, even if I feel like I deserve it.
○ Strongly disagree
○ Disagree
○ Agree
○ Strongly agree

4. I avoid difficult people.
○ Strongly disagree
○ Disagree
○ Agree
○ Strongly agree

5. I avoid confrontation.
○ Strongly disagree
○ Disagree
○ Agree
○ Strongly agree

6. I am usually the leader of the group.
○ Strongly disagree
○ Disagree
○ Agree
○ Strongly agree

7. I spend most of my time trying to please others.
○ Strongly disagree
○ Disagree
○ Agree
○ Strongly agree

8. I feel confident.
○ Strongly disagree
○ Disagree
○ Agree
○ Strongly agree

9. I feel comfortable disagreeing with someone in a position of authority.
- ○ Strongly disagree
- ○ Disagree
- ○ Agree
- ○ Strongly agree

10. I often regret not saying certain things after having been in an argument.
- ○ Strongly disagree
- ○ Disagree
- ○ Agree
- ○ Strongly agree

11. I get nervous speaking in front of groups of people.
- ○ Strongly disagree
- ○ Disagree
- ○ Agree
- ○ Strongly agree

12. I have a hard time saying "No" to people.
- ○ Strongly disagree
- ○ Disagree
- ○ Agree
- ○ Strongly agree

13. I'd rather not make returns or exchanges even if my merchandise is damaged/ill-fitting.
- ○ Strongly disagree
- ○ Disagree

○ Agree
○ Strongly agree

14. I would rather take the blame than argue.
○ Strongly disagree
○ Disagree
○ Agree
○ Strongly agree

15. I tend to get nervous near celebrities and attractive people.
○ Strongly disagree
○ Disagree
○ Agree
○ Strongly agree

Scoring:
For each "Strongly Disagree" give yourself **3 points.**
For each "Disagree" give yourself **2 point.**
For each "Agree" give yourself **1 point.**
For each "Strongly Agree" give yourself **0 points.**

TOTAL SCORE OF 0–15
TURN IT UP!

TOTAL SCORE OF 16–30
JUST RIGHT!

TOTAL SCORE OF 31–45
TURN IT DOWN!

The Nely Switch

On *Celebrity Apprentice*, Donald Trump assembled a unique group of all-star celebrities from the areas of sports, television, modeling, etc. On that show, I met a woman who wowed me with her switch savvy. For that reason, I call Nely Galán the Ultimate Switch.

This Latina media dynamo has launched ten television channels internationally, served as the former president of Telemundo, marketed and promoted blue-chip brands in the United States and Latin America, and produced over 600 episodes of television shows in English and Spanish, including the FOX hit reality show *The Swan*. She's got quite a sophisticated switch, and I mean that as the sincerest of compliments!

On *Celebrity Apprentice* she was able to win the trust of the most egotistical man ever to enter Trump's boardroom: Gene Simmons, star of his own show on A&E, *Gene Simmons Family Jewels,* and singer/ founder of the rock group KISS. Most of the women were offended by Gene's misogynistic approach to project management. But not Nely. She modulated her bSwitch and won not only his trust but also his confidence. In the end, Gene knew Nely would be fired if she ever stepped foot in that boardroom—so, during his time as project manager, thanks to Gene, she never had to.

Not only is Nely—and her use of her bSwitch—an excellent model for Latina women, but she has set a shining example for women everywhere!

"Everybody's Somebody's BITCH."

W.W.O.D.

Hi, Omarosa,
I just started a new job, and I'm having a tough time figuring out my place in the food chain. Here's the thing: Saying "thanks" and "please" and "yes" has made me the office bitch (as in lackey). But the minute I make even the simplest demand—"Do this" or "Do that"—I become the office bitch (as in…angry black woman no one invites to happy hour on Friday night). Is there a happy medium? I haven't been able to find one yet, but maybe you could help a girlfriend out….

Best,
Angela

Dear Angela,
Don't be afraid of the power you gain after turning on the switch. If you show those around you that you are confident and comfortable in your position, they will be more likely to take your word as THE word. The truth is, by saying "Do this" and "Do that" you are giving off a sense of authority and showing that you've grown and are ready for more challenges—a great thing! Soon enough you'll be leading your department, then your company. Sure, you might not get invited out for Friday-night margaritas, but you'll be wining and dining with high-rollers and heavy-hitters in no time.

Good luck!
Omarosa

* * *

Hi, Omarosa,
I feel pretty self-assured and aware of who I am and what I want. I've been employing a sort of Bitch Switch my whole life. The problem is: I'm not exactly seeing any results. I've been promoted twice in the past five years, which is great, but...I want to be the PRESIDENT of my company, not a VP my whole life. It's kind of like "always the bridesmaid, never the bride," but at work. And like I said, it's not for lack of trying. What's up with that?

From one bitch to another,
Kendra

Dear Kendra,
It sounds like you're doing everything right. So what's the problem? NOTHING! No one gets tapped to be the president of ANYTHING overnight. It takes a lot of blood, sweat, and tears...and, yes, bitching. There were times in my life when I was working too hard to eat or sleep, but I kept persevering and here I am! There is no set "timeline" for success—there is no set path to follow. You know the saying, "Keep up the good work"? Well, it works!

Good luck!
Omarosa

Bitch Switch Tips!

- A woman who is confident is less of a bitch. She's also less likely to bitch.
- A woman who is confident has little need of outside validation. She defines for herself who she is.
- A woman who is confident has no need to belittle or demean others.
- Pleasing will hold you back!
- GOOD, BETTER, BEST—never let it rest, till your GOOD is BETTER and your BETTER is BEST!
- Don't look to others to make you happy or to provide you joy.
- Acquire a CAN-DO attitude, not a CAN'T-DO attitude!
- Be consistent!
- It does not matter what others think of you— only what you think of YOURSELF!

PART III

Leading with
THE SWITCH

"The thing women have yet to
learn is nobody gives you power.
You just take it."

–Roseanne Barr

Who's the Boss? YOU'RE THE BOSS

*"A woman is like a teabag. It's only when she's
in hot water that you realize how strong she is."*
—Nancy Reagan

The next critical step in developing your bSwitch is developing your leadership style. Your ability (or inability) to be a strong leader in your own life will greatly affect how you view the world and how the world views you. During my lectures and seminars I am often asked for my advice about effective leadership. The tough reality about leadership is that everybody wants to be boss, but no one wants to do the hard, necessary things that being a boss requires!

I've studied leadership extensively, and the key element that most of the world's great leaders share is that they are able to take heat and make difficult decisions. They are decisive and free themselves from the shackles of doubt, fear, and "what-ifs" that hold others back. They have no problem making a tough decision and letting the chips fall where they may. They don't worry about those who second-guess their decisions. They have developed a unique style of leadership that serves them well when they are in the hot seat!

"I HAVE MET MY SHE-RO AND SHE IS ME!"

On a daily basis, we are faced with a barrage of minor annoyances and confrontations. You may find your bSwitch helpful at times and not so much at other times. You will have to discern when it is appropriate to turn the bSwitch on and off without blowing a fuse. You don't want to burn out by constantly riling yourself up, because it takes a great deal of energy to flip the switch on. As with an actual light switch, you use plenty of electricity when it's on. It's not wise to leave it burning twenty-four hours a day. As you assemble your bSwitch, your ability to lead will come very naturally.

Case in point: Turning on the Bitch Switch only means that there is a different, stronger way to respond than the one you're used to. You do have options, and you can speak up for yourself. Once you have resolved whatever issue is troubling you, the switch can be flipped back down till the next time you need it. The tools of leadership and focus must be in place for you to access when and if you need them!

W.W.O.D.

Miss O,
I'm in kind of a dilemma and I thought you could help.

Two months ago I informed my boss that I needed to take a week off to attend my best friend's wedding in Italy. He told me that would be fine IF we had wrapped up the yearlong project I've been heading. I've been working my butt off these past two weeks to finish things up, but it's just not going to happen! I've already bought my ticket to Italy, and I can't let my best friend down, but I'm afraid I'm going to get fired if I just leave the country.

What do you think I should do? I've hardly been able to sleep at night worrying about this.

Sincerely,
Sleepless (really) in Seattle

Dear Sleepless,
I learned this lesson pretty easily, but it never ceases to amaze me how many women let WORRYING affect their lives for the worse! Of course worrying will cause you to lose sleep—it will also affect your personal relationships, your appetite, and your overall well-being. Do yourself a favor and stop WORRYING now. What's the worst that can happen? You've done absolutely everything right: telling your boss in advance that you would need to take time off and working as hard as you humanly can to finish up this project. Your vacation seems well-deserved. Give your boss a status report before you leave to PROVE just how well-deserved, and you might be pleasantly surprised by a raise when you return!

Good luck!
Omarosa

SHE in the Land of HE

"Toughness doesn't have to come in a pinstripe suit."
-Dianne Feinstein

A man who is a leader is called a visionary; a woman who is a leader is called a BITCH! This very concept keeps women from enthusiastically ascending to leadership positions. Most women managers are unable to recognize, embrace, or utilize their power and advance their own ambitions. The truth is that leadership is not encouraged, nurtured, or celebrated. By keeping the bSwitch cut off or low women perceive that they will attain a certain approval by or acceptance into the "good ol' boy" network. There are women who think the only way to get accepted is by emulating their male counterparts. They become club-swingin', cigar-smokin', whiskey-swiggin' women who trade their femininity for acceptance.

But when it comes down to it, women are wired differently than men. Our emotional levels are set to a higher degree than men's. My infamous quote from the first season of *The Apprentice* was, "I'm not here to make friends." This statement was perceived by many as icy and emotionless. When one of my male counterparts made a similar statement, however, it was left on the editing room floor because it wasn't considered particularly noteworthy. Friendship just was not my first priority on the show. I was there to win the dream job of a lifetime with Donald Trump. It was important for me to remove emotion from the equation and place myself on a level playing field with both the male and female contestants. In the opening credits of our show, there's a phrase, "It's not PERSONAL, just BUSINESS," that flashes across the screen. But with women, it's always personal!

On *The Apprentice* the teams were divided by gender, so I thought I had a great strategy: I envisioned that the women would band together and pick off the men one by one. Unfortunately, the women were paralyzed by petty disagreements over who liked them and who didn't. There was so much infighting between the women that we couldn't focus on our tasks.

Men have successfully used this desire on the part of women to be liked to manipulate women and restrict their growth and advancement. The men on the show perpetuated these negative stereotypes for their own advancement. A very easy way for the men's team to have camaraderie was for them to say to one another, "Wow, she's a bitch," and sort of bond over that. Women perpetuate this, too; they do more damage to each other in this regard. Even back in 2003, I realized that the female project managers on *The Apprentice* were in a no-win situation. What these women needed was BITCH SWITCH training.

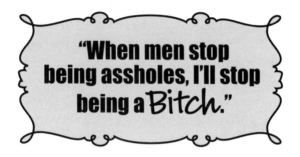

"When men stop being assholes, I'll stop being a *Bitch*."

I can admit that as a young executive starting out I committed myself to going out to learn how to play poker and golf and trying to fit in with the good ol' boys. At the time, I did not see it as trading in my most valuable trait— being a woman! Women cannot afford to discount the good ol' boy network in any organization; it's not going away anytime soon. But these days I do it my way—I golf in a miniskirt and close the biggest deals in the highest heels.

The Twit Switch

The difference between turning on the Twit Switch, as I call it, and the Bitch Switch, is that the bSwitch is a more empowering way of accomplishing goals and getting what you want. The Twit Switch is for the weak; it's nothing more than putting power in other people's hands and hoping they'll respond or react favorably to your feminine wiles. I am not denying that it can work, but it's a very frivolous way to act.

A perfect example of this kind of behavior was when I was on *Celebrity Apprentice* with supermodel Carol Alt, a woman whom I repeatedly called out on this kind of behavior, much to her dismay. Every time a man walked into the room she fluttered and cooed and batted her lashes at him. She said things like, "Oh, I'm going to learn as much as I can from you!" She would have been so much more respected and effective had she just taken the attitude, "I'm in this game to win. What can I learn from you to help with that?" She painted herself as—or really is, I'm not sure—silly, trivial, and weak, by turning on the Twit Switch.

I truly believe that so many women act this way not because it's been particularly helpful or effective for them in the past, but because they don't know enough about acting any other way! There is no dialogue about the bSwitch. Women don't have to be childish and flirtatious when they get pulled over, pulling that whole number, "Oh, Officer, was I speeding? I just didn't realize, silly me! Oh, I really can't get a ticket!"

How about a straightforward, "Officer, was I really going that fast?"

If you want to *Bitch* about something please take a number.

W.W.O.D.

Hello,
Firstly, I wanted to say I'm so impressed by your professionalism at all times, Omarosa. It always seems you are dressed appropriately and attractively, and that's something I struggle with myself. I'm working for a stock brokerage firm—in their research department—and I'm discouraged by the lack of women executives in the company. I'm surrounded by chauvinistic, meat-n-potatoes, sports-fanatical men all day and get shot down every time I offer an idea, which is typically stolen right out from under me. I've been considering switching professions, because I just can't seem to make myself known in this company. I feel like that's giving up, but I honestly don't know what else to do. Help?

Dear Help,
Think like a man! It sounds crazy (and might feel crazy at first) but you'll be amazed at what an impact it will have. You'll be amazed by the impact YOU will have! At one point, it's not about who's wearing a skirt and whose golf handicap is better. Don't be afraid of the B-word...use your switch! If the men around you have been "stealing" your ideas, make damn sure YOU are the one to bring it to your boss. Then YOU are the one who will get the credit. Don't take their "shooting you down" personally. Be confident and strong in your opinions. The way you see yourself is the way that you're seen. You go, girl.

Good luck!
Omarosa

All You Need Is the Walk, the Wave, and the Attitude!

"Life's under no obligation to give us what we expect."
-Margaret Mitchell

Much of my leadership style comes from my time as an athlete in high school and college. There I learned the value of teamwork, dedication, perseverance and, yes, leadership. Research has shown that nearly four out of five successful women executives played sports during their youth. The bSwitch is very much like sports. When you walk on the court you put on your game face, you formulate your strategy, and you play to win. After the game is over, and you have marked a W or L in the column, for win or loss, you put away your game face and you reflect on the lessons from the game.

During these competitive days I was not concerned about being perceived as too aggressive; I was just focused on the WIN. Well, the same goes for the bSwitch. You turn it on when you need to (game face on) and you turn it off when you don't!

In addition to sports I competed in beauty pageants throughout my high school and college years. Being a titleholder taught me many lessons. The greatest lesson came from my very first pageant: the Miss Buckeye Elk pageant.

I was introduced to pageants by a woman who has remained a close friend and mentor to me to this day. My high school librarian, Jocelyn Dabney, received a flyer announcing a local beauty pageant. She gave me the flyer and encouraged me to enter. Ms. Dabney thought that I was a pretty girl with lots of potential, but was way too tomboyish and aggressive. A pageant, she thought, would be a good way to round me out and smooth out some of the rough edges. I entered the pageant with no training or understanding of what it would take to win. I chose baton twirling as my talent because I was head majorette for my high school marching band, the Rayen High Tigers.

I stumbled across the stage for most of the pageant and tried to do what we discussed during rehearsals. I did my best and placed first runner-up. The winner of the pageant would go on to represent our local lodge at the state level. Although I did not bring home the crown on that first attempt, I definitely learned my lesson:

FAILURE WAS NOT AN OPTION FOR ME!

Watching the girl who won take her victory stroll with the crown, sash, and that ridiculous wave was a very disconcerting feeling. Losing was the best motivator for me. Had I won on that first attempt, I am certain that I would never have tried to learn how to properly compete and win in that arena. Rejection is not a good feeling for anyone, even when you have strong armor, like I do. However, for me, failure is not an option. I like the challenge when somebody tells me, "No, you're not prepared." I walked away from that situation FIRED UP with newfound determination. "I will go out and take classes, improve my skills, get the relevant experience—whatever it takes. I will figure out how to become Miss Buckeye Elk," I vowed right then and there, at that critical moment, as I stood on stage feeling what losing was all about.

HWPO—Hard Work Pays Off

"I catnap now and then, but I think while I nap, so it's not a waste of time." -Martha Stewart

Competing in beauty pageants, I came to realize this fact of life: The reality is that there will always be someone who CAN do what you CAN'T do! There will always be someone taller than you. For sure there will be someone skinnier than you. There will be girls more talented and much richer than you. Some will be smarter. This is a simple fact of life, and none of that is going to change. **But the one great equalizer will always be hard work and**

perseverance. I went back and won the Miss Buckeye Elk title the next year as I'd promised myself I would do, and also went on to win at the state level.

I've attributed my success solely to *hard work, commitment to my goal, and perseverance.*

"SETBACKS ARE SETUPS FOR COMEBACKS!"
–Willie Jolley

ADDITIONAL NOTABLE
PAGEANT TITLES INCLUDE:
MISS YOUNGSTOWN, 1992
MISS CENTRAL STATE
UNIVERSITY, 1995
AND
MRS. DISTRICT OF
COLUMBIA, 2001

W.W.O.D.

Dear Omarosa,
All my life my very conservative family has told me to "sit straight," "don't speak unless you have been spoken to," "chew with your mouth closed"—you get the point. Yes, these are important rules of etiquette, but I've always felt meek and mousy compared to the other girls in the room. I do what I'm told, but I don't stand out.

I think I need a good dose of bitchiness. Where should I start?

Thanks a lot,
Miss Manners

Dear Ms. Manners,
There's nothing wrong with having manners and being polite, but now, understandably, you feel like a wallflower—BECAUSE YOU'VE MADE YOURSELF A WALLFLOWER! Here are some tips I learned from being in pageants that will help you bring out your inner bitch and make you shine in no time: SMILE when it's appropriate! Your "stage presence" is everything! Be true to yourself! Figure out what your positive traits are and USE THEM! Worry about YOU, not the COMPETITION! Don't be afraid to ask for advice!

Form opinions on EVERYTHING…and voice them! Be prepared to win OR lose!

Good luck!
Omarosa

Taming of the Shrew

"When I'm good I'm very, very good,
but when I'm bad, I'm better." –Mae West

Another area of my youth that I drew much of my leadership style from was my years in theater. After a couple of semesters of drama classes at Rayen High School, I auditioned for the prestigious Youngstown Playhouse. My first major production was a Black History Month presentation called *Steal Away Home*. I played the role of a mother who was forced to send her son north on the Underground Railroad in order to provide for him a better life. This mother gave words of encouragement to her young child and one of the last things she told him was that "some things just have to be done, son." She made a difficult decision that in fact changed their course of history.

The next school year, I joined a local youth drama troupe called the Shakespeare Sampler, and we performed many of the great works of Shakespeare. I vividly recall how enthusiastically I auditioned for the role of Katherine in *The Taming of the Shrew*. My directors said that I was a natural to play the intelligent, outspoken, and ill-tempered "shrew" named Kate. What the director saw in me that I did not see in myself was a knack for turning it on and turning it off! In our table reads, I often questioned Petruchio's efforts to "tame" Kate. I thought that it might break her spirit and change the essence of who she was. After all, being a shrew is not always a bad thing.

In my second year with the Shakespeare Sampler, I was thrilled to land the role of the infamous Lady Macbeth. Uttering her powerful, wicked lines—*"These deeds must not be thought after these ways; so, it will make us mad"*—made me feel invincible. The genesis of my villain character on reality TV was derived from these strong archetypes.

My mom once asked me why I never auditioned for the role of Juliet. I explained to her, in the way only a fourteen-year-old could, that I thought Juliet was a fool to give up so much of herself for that "Romeo dude." I refused to even play such a weak and gullible character.

My background as a thespian, athlete, and competitive beauty gave me a huge leadership advantage when I appeared on *The Apprentice* and every other reality show since then.

"GIVE YOURSELF AN ADVANTAGE IN LIFE.
TAKE A RISK & REAP THE REWARDS."

Fake It Till You Make It

"Assume a virtue if you have it not."
—William Shakespeare

Way back when I was just a teen, I had instinctively mastered a very important element of the bSwitch, which can be summarized as FAKE IT TILL YOU MAKE IT. It's nothing more than separating the action from the feeling. Many women believe that they have to feel a certain way, and *then* they'll act a certain way, allowing emotion to drive their actions. That's like putting the cart before the horse. This is what drives destructive "someday" thinking. For example, "Someday, I will feel skinny, then I'll lose twenty pounds. I'll wear those jeans I bought and go there and do this...." That theory of emotion-then-action is FLAWED.

I am here to testify to the power of going through the motions—just as if you already accomplished that evasive goal of the promotion you desire, the salary you desire, the clout and respect that you dream of! Take the action first, before the feelings are in place! Fake it till you make it—you will be amazed at the results!

A Bully Is No Match for your BITCH SWITCH!

"You're either giving ulcers, or getting them."
—Steve Ogunro

When you lead with the bSwitch, you are certain to face opposition in your personal life and at work. These types of roadblocks come with the territory of leadership development. But sometimes you will encounter a situation that has the potential to stop you dead in your tracks.

During my time working as Director of Education and Research for Dr. Bill and Camille Cosby's nonprofit organization, the National Visionary Leadership Project (NVLP), I encountered a phenomenon that I have come to recognize as Workplace Bullying. The bully in this situation did not target me, but the psycho-bitch tormented many of my colleagues. Yes, this bully was a woman! Contrary to popular belief, women can be bullies, too. In fact, women-to-women bullying makes up 50 percent of all workplace bullying!

Many of the victims who were on the receiving end of her wrath would come into my office, shut the door, and share their war stories with me. They often questioned, "Why me?" They did not understand why the bully never really focused her venom at ME, Lady O. The simple reason was that this bully was no match for my **Bitch Switch!**

There seemed to be no end to her campaign of terror. She would use tactics that are commonly used by workplace bullies. Her weapons of choice were psychological torment and salient harassment. Many of her victims could be classified as doormats or shrinking violets. She would target these people, men and women, making some random off-the-wall demand or taking plain-and-simple cheap shots that were way out of line. She was not above lying and creating false accusations to professionally and personally destroy the weaklings in her path. But she was wise enough not to mess with me because of my powerful bSwitch.

BITCH SWITCH EXERCISE

How to recognize if that BITCH is a BULLY... and if so how the BITCH SWITCH CAN HELP!

Are you apprehensive about going into the office? Are you completely stressed out during your workday? Do you get physically ill with anxiety anticipating the next attack?

Read the Top 10 Bully Tactics below and ✔check off all that apply to YOUR workplace nemesis, then keep reading to check out strategies on how to DEFEND yourself against him/her:

[Check as many as apply]

Does your nemesis:

1. __ Blame you for "errors"
2. __ Make unreasonable job demands
3. __ Criticize your ability
4. __ Show inconsistent compliance with rules
5. __ Threaten you with job loss
6. __ Insult you
7. __ Discount/deny your accomplishments
8. __ Exclude you, "ice you out"
9. __ Yell, scream
10. __ Take credit for your work

How to Use the bSwitch to Stop Bullies Dead in Their Tracks!

"I found my inner bitch and ran with her."
—Courtney Love

The first step to stopping a bully is FLIPPING YOUR SWITCH! Stop whining and worrying and get ready to fight fire with fire. It's not your fault that you are being targeted by some mean, self-absorbed, paranoid, narcissistic FREAK—that's just WHO BULLIES ARE! You are going to have to summon all of the courage and strength that you have inside and be prepared to battle.

In the case of my colleagues at NVLP, they spent hours and days around the water cooler pondering why this witch was targeting THEM. I advised my coworkers not to waste time trying to figure out the bully's motivations. Bullies tend to act this way because they get a thrill out of seeing your fear and insecurities. They keep doing it because they are looking for another power "fix" that they get out of making you sweat. They are bullies for many reasons, which could include their desire to simply manipulate and exploit people they perceive as weak.

In this example the bully happened to be the boss, but your bully could take on the form of a peer, manager, or even subordinate. Whoever your tormenter is, you're going to have to set your fear and anxiety aside to put an end to your misery.

bSwitch Tip #1 Call a spade a spade, or in this case, a bully a bully. Confront bullies by informing them that what they are doing is detrimental and HAS TO STOP.

bSwitch Tip #2 Document your abuse! Every time an incident happens, make a note of it so that you can show that there is a pattern to the destructive behavior.

bSwitch Tip #3 Report them to Human Resources, keeping in mind that HR's role is not that of counseling agency. Your trip to HR will be part of your documentation of the abuse.

bSwitch Tip #4 Find an advocate—you may consult an attorney or a neutral party within the organization who can help validate your concerns and help end the pain.

bSwitch Tip #5 If you're faced with an extreme case of bullying, you may find that your only option is to cut your losses and leave. It may be the only way to salvage what's left of your physical and mental health. A SPECIAL NOTE TO DOORMATS: Unless you learn how and when to flip your switch, no matter where you go, there WILL be a bully and you WILL be the target! In these cases, quitting isn't going to solve anything. Your only insurance against bullying is to boldly flip your bSwitch!

Workplace bullies can ruin your life—if you let them. This section was designed to help you combat your bully and make it to the top, where you belong. And for any future bullies out there, make note of these tips to end your bullying ways. According to the Workplace Bullying Institute's 2007 Zogby Survey, the first and largest national poll about the prevalence and nature of workplace bullying in the United States, 37 percent of U.S. workers have been personally bullied—that is 54 million Americans! An additional 12 percent have witnessed it. See the report summary in the appendix for more fascinating stats.

W.W.O.D.

Dear Omarosa,
My boss is a tyrant: cold, demanding, and unbreakable.
When I had finally had ENOUGH of being his "personal"
slave, I decided to speak up. I went in for a one-on-one with
him feeling strong, confident, almost invincible. But after
only one sentence of my manifesto I could feel him staring
and studying my every move. I buckled under the pressure
and completely broke down crying. I had to leave the room,
completely humiliated, with my confidence shattered. What
happened?

Sincerely,
Sobbing Sally

Dear Sally,
I hate to admit this, but since it happened to me in
front of twenty million viewers during my firing on
the first season of The Apprentice, I will share.

Sometimes you're going to CRY.

When your emotions get the best of you, and you get
sick and tired of being sick and tired, it just happens.
Hopefully it does not happen in front of your boss (as
in your case) or in front of all of America (as in my
case). Sally, a good cry is very therapeutic and may
have been what you needed to wake up.

Be careful not to turn your bSwitch down so low that you lose control over your emotions. Remember, there is a time and place for everything. Don't beat yourself up. It happens to the best of us.

I SHARE because I CARE,
Omarosa

Managing Fear and Anxiety

"You gain strength, courage, and confidence by every experience in which you really stop to look fear in the face." -Eleanor Roosevelt

Fear, anxiety, and frustration—like the fear, anxiety, and frustration that workplace bullies can give you—become all-consuming emotions that will HOLD YOU BACK from what you really aspire to do! It's important that you use the power of the bSwitch to eliminate these. The problem with holding in these emotions, allowing anger to build up, is that it wears you down physically. You can't make it to the top if you're too exhausted to get there! The anxiety and stress that build up, along with all the held-back words and actions that eventually lead to a blow-up, are not worth it. That constant biting-back affects every one of your faculties, not to mention your nerves and your peace of mind. It destroys your ability to do other, more productive things.

It's like holding toxins inside of yourself when you allow a powder keg of resentment and anger to grow. It only takes one spark to cause a huge explosion, and that BOOM! may not necessarily hit the person who caused all your stress to begin with! Everybody—but most of all YOU—suffers when you hold your emotions inside. Just let them out early, at the time they pop up, because they will come out—one way or another.

Before you go any further on this path to mastering your very own bSwitch, you must know, and believe, this:

The bSwitch will ONLY work when you get to the point where you have had ENOUGH of being a punching bag for everyone in your life, when you have the courage to stop being the doormat that your boss and other bullies wipe their feet on every day of the week. Remember: **You are not the receptacle for everyone's mess, and you most definitely were not put on earth to be a punching bag for ANYONE!**

Bitch Switch Tips!

- Make difficult decisions and MOVE ON!
- Use your switch when you need a NEW, STRONGER response to obstacles in your way. After you've resolved that issue, flip it back down!
- It's not personal, it's just business!
- Failure isn't your last option—it's NEVER an option...PERIOD!
- Fake it till you make it!

PART IV

Communicating With
THE SWITCH

"If there is anything in the world more annoying than having people talk about you, it is certainly having no one talk about you." –Oscar Wilde

COMMUNICATION 101: The Power of Nommo

"It's not what I do, but the way I do it. It's not what I say, but the way I say it." -Mae West

What is it you want out of life?

The very first step is to articulate your desires. You have to communicate your dreams for them to even start to exist, much less materialize! Your dreams can't just be blurry visions in your head. You have to communicate them clearly, concisely, and thoroughly.

When I was at Howard University, the historically black college in Washington, D.C., I took a class in human communications with Dr. Richard Wright. There I learned a powerful concept that comes from ancient African religion: the concept of Nommo. Nommo can be summarized as *"the life force of the word."* The Dogon people of Africa believed that words were so powerful that the ones they chose to utter could influence all the events and circumstances of their lives.

Nommo is about not only achieving your desires but also effectively communicating them. The spoken word involves engaging the speaker and puts you in control of your own life—and destiny. The concept of Nommo has transformative power—meaning it can change your life for the better—but starts with the spoken word!

The Dogon people believed that through the spoken word, and Nommo, people could build better human relationships. This is a connection that doesn't exist, for example, in the WRITTEN word (in e-mails and memos). There is a power in being PRESENT and physically VOCALIZING your thoughts and commands. You can practice Nommo today by using your bSwitch to put your dreams and desires into words—then put those words into action.

Communicating your expectations of how you should be treated is the very heart of what the Bitch Switch is all about. If you improve your communication skills, and take some of the advice in this book to heart, you really can change your life!

The Power of Positive Daily Affirmations

"So you begin making your way through the 'reality of today' rather than holding out for the 'promise of tomorrow.'" -"The Awakening"

We've already discussed a little about how communicating your desires can change your life. But how does it connect to the bSwitch? The bSwitch is about turning it on and off. During self-development and reflection, your bSwitch should be somewhat dimmed or turned very low—you are opening your mind to new possibilities.

After the White House I worked as a freelancer for CNN. This was during the Time Warner merger and lots of people were being fired. Bernard Shaw was retiring, and Judy Woodruff and Greta Van Susteren were key anchors. During these difficult days in the newsroom, when friends were being axed left and right, I used personal daily affirmations to get through. Affirmations are uplifting statements about something personal you want to achieve. My daily affirmations allowed me to cope with extreme stress and anxiety that I was dealing with. At the time I knew that I did not want to stay at CNN longer than a year, so I would affirm: "I CAN survive anything as long as I know it won't last forever." In fact, I started a countdown to the day that I would be moving on to the next chapter of my life. "Eleven months till I start my own firm." I would also affirm that "God never gives us more than we can deal with."

Every day I would write my affirmation in my planner and repeat it silently to myself. The power of repetition allowed me to counteract many of my negative thoughts about the things that were going on during this "corporate downsizing." I was able to keep a positive outlook even as the number of employees dwindled and the workload increased.

Although there are many books on affirmations (one of my favorites is *Until Today! Daily Devotions for Spiritual Growth and Peace of Mind* by Iyanla Vanzant), the affirmations that we create from our own experiences are the most effective.

When I was preparing for my first acting role on *Passions*, the NBC soap opera, I was very nervous. I grew up watching soaps with my aunties, and felt the magnitude of this milestone in my personal journey. I created the affirmation: "This is my role, and my moment, and I will shine. On this day, I am a star, and I have the ability to shine brightly." Behind my words, I added conviction and belief to what I was saying. **With affirmations, you can turn things that you hope are possible into things that you know are probable.**

When I was selected to be a celebrity participant on the game show *One vs. One Hundred,* I remember that my affirmation for the taping was very simple yet profound: "I am smarter than the rest. I will be the last person standing, because I am the best."

It's important that YOU create your own personal affirmations and speak them every day. One of my favorites is called *The Awakening* (there is an ongoing debate as to who the originator of *The Awakening* truly is—as that debate is ongoing, we are proud to use the lessons in this moving and truly inspirational piece). I used to have each of my students read this affirmation aloud in various classes that I taught because it is a great step to opening your mind to the possibilities of transforming yourself. Try this paragraph now; the complete version of *The Awakening* can be found in the back of this book.

> *There comes a time in your life when you finally get it.... When in the midst of all your fears and insanity you stop dead in your tracks and somewhere the voice inside your head cries out: ENOUGH! Enough fighting and crying or struggling to hold on. And You become like a child quieting down after a blind tantrum. Your sobs begin to subside, you shudder once or twice, you blink back your tears, and through a mantle of wet lashes you begin to look at the world through new eyes. This is your awakening.*

BITCH SWITCH EXERCISE
PERSONAL AFFIRMATION

Now it's your turn to create your personal affirmations! Read my examples below, and then use the space provided to create your own.

Motivating Affirmations:
I am deserving of all the good things in my life.
If I make mistakes, I will give myself the benefit of the doubt.

_____

_____

Health and Wellness Affirmations:
I know what it takes to be healthy.
I will do whatever it takes to stay healthy.

_____

_____

Personal Finance:
I am wealthy and abundant.
I create abundance in all that I say and do.

_____

_____

Career Affirmations:
I am successful.
My success allows me to create opportunities for me and those around me.

_____

_____

Personal Relationship Affirmations:
I know how to build strong, long-lasting relationships.
I am a confident and positive person who attracts good people.

_____

_____

Bitch Switch Communication ESSENTIALS!

"I succeeded by saying what everyone else is thinking."
-Joan Rivers

Beyond your goals, communication is a central part of how you present yourself at work, in relationships, and at home. There are several essential keys to communication that you *must* focus on when using your Bitch Switch. Following these will ensure that you find success in whatever you do!

• Self-confidence is the number one skill!

Self-confidence is the key to locating your bSwitch and effectively communicating. Before you even open your mouth to utter your first word you must believe in what you're saying; that will impact how the listener receives your message. If you are not confident in what you're saying, then you will undermine your credibility and POWER.

• Use words that communicate authority.

There are words that help establish you as a powerhouse and there are words that scream WEAK! Eliminate words such as "I think" and "I feel" from your statements. Flip on the switch and use language that packs a punch—not that weakens your message.

- **Be clear, concise, and thorough.**

My journalism professor at Central State University, Dr. Emil Dansker, taught me that the most effective way to communicate was to try to achieve CCT. Strive to make sure that your message is clear (not ambiguous), concise (always to the point), and thorough (make sure that you effectively convey your message).

- **Speak at a good pace and be sure to enunciate.**

It's extremely important that you don't speak too fast when you're nervous or too slow when you are intimidated. Pay close attention to the last syllable in every word. Practice your message delivery in front of a mirror and find the pace that best suits your communication style.

- **Develop good listening skills.**

Know when to turn the switch off and shut up! Listening is essential in avoiding misunderstanding and discerning expectations.

- **Assume the role of expert and use facts and data to support your opinion.**

Become an SME (subject matter expert). When you know your stuff, it's easy to speak confidently, and others will be eager to hear what you have to say!

• Always be logical in your communication.

Try to organize your thoughts before you speak. If it does not make sense to you, then it's definitely not going to make sense to others. Use common sense when responding under pressure. And remember K.I.S.S.—Keep It Simple, Stupid.

• Try to incorporate goal-oriented language.

Communicate with a clear goal in mind. Clearly state your expectations and outline deliverables for you and your listeners.

• Avoid unnecessary storytelling.

As women we have a tendency to want to disclose intimate information about ourselves when we get nervous. But it's important to consider the environment and circumstances before sharing personal stories.

• Don't sugarcoat your comments.

In communication we call this hedging, or adding unnecessary statements before making a request. Avoid sugarcoating at all cost. It muddies the waters of communication and makes it difficult to separate your demands from your emotions.

• Give direct and honest feedback.

If asked for your opinion, try your best to provide useful information. Don't state what you think the other person might want to HEAR. This does not help you or the person you're giving the false information to.

• Speak assertively but not harshly.

Communicate in a way that shows that you mean business. This is the best way to be taken seriously by your coworkers or associates.

• Use language that's familiar to your listener.

Don't try to outdo others with big words or concepts that are not appropriate to the situation. Develop a communication style that is malleable and can be used in varied situations.

• Become a good conversationalist by keeping up with current events.

It helps to know what's going on in the world and to state your opinion or point of view on such issues. Your ability to speak on a wider array of topics will make you a much better conversationalist and help you in uncomfortable situations.

THE BITCH SWITCH COMMUNICATION CHART

Question	Non-Assertive TURN IT UP!	Assertive JUST RIGHT	Aggressive TONE IT DOWN!
What are you working on?	"Well, um...I'm trying to complete all of the projects that have piled up on me this week. And, um...then I'll get to that other stuff that's been backing up...and, um...." Doormats are vague and general. Doormats ramble.	"Why do you ask?" Never volunteer more information than necessary. Determine a person's motivation for asking, then decide what information is being requested. In the White House we used to operate on an NTKB (Need to Know Basis). Decide who needs to know and for what purpose. And understand that certain disclosures can and will be used to exploit you or a situation in the future. Focus on being clear, concise, and thorough! Keep it short, curt, and icy. The more attitude, the more impact!	"More than you, I'm sure." Stay away from accusations (like this) and other "You" messages. Putting others down, giving no recognition, and using subjective, superior wording will make you come across as a DICTATOR! Stay in the neutral; be clear and objective.

Question	Non-Assertive **TURN IT UP!**	Assertive **JUST RIGHT**	Aggressive **TONE IT DOWN!**
Can you turn in that report by the end of the day?	"Well, sir, I am...um, I will try." "Ok, I will try to do that!"	"Well, Bob, I am focused on the year-end projections. Do you mind waiting on that? I have a lot to do." Utilize the authority's name to eliminate the distance between you and the boss. "Fine!" The bSwitch allows you to close out a conversation leaving no question about your displeasure of the task at hand.	"Does it matter? Brenda is going to take all of the credit anyway." Being sarcastic and blaming or labeling others are signs of aggressive verbal behavior.
	Doormats speak tentatively and kowtow to those in authority. Using "apologetic words" is self-defeating.		
Do you mind taking on this one extra thing?	"Oh, no, I don't mind. I can just **move some things around to make it work.**" Weak terminology and an apologetic tone discredit your words!	"I can't take another thing on at this time." Get rid of the need to please. Don't lie about what you can and cannot do. Set limits and don't be afraid to face the consequences. (Nine times out of ten they will go find a doormat to take on their work!)	"ANOTHER project? ARE YOU KIDDING ME? I'M STRESSED ENOUGH AS IT IS!" Using shrill, loud, or tense tones signifies that you are not in control of yourself.

Question	Non-Assertive TURN IT UP!	Assertive JUST RIGHT	Aggressive TONE IT DOWN!
I didn't know you were so busy! Why didn't you just say so?	"I thought your would notice that I am stretched to my limit right now. Couldn't you sense it?" Stop assuming that people will read your mind! They won't dare, 'cause they don't care! They only want what is best for them at that moment. They don't care about what it takes to get it done. They just want it done. You have speak up and not rely on clairvoyance to communicate your feelings.	If you use your bSwitch appropriately, you won't have to worry about this situation with your coworkers and bosses! Always be up-front when you are feeling overworked or overwhelmed.	"You didn't ask!" Don't wait for those around you to ASK you how you feel—they probably never will!

Question	Non-Assertive **TURN IT UP!**	Assertive **JUST RIGHT**	Aggressive **TONE IT DOWN!**
Ms. Violet, what do you think about the direction that we are going in?	"Well I...um...am not sure. I guess it's all right." A doormat finds herself at a loss for words when put on the spot about her feelings, thoughts, likes, or dislikes. If this describes you, you have to stop worrying and start flipping on the bSwitch!	"I don't think we're focusing on the future. I have some great ideas on how we could improve. I'd love to discuss them with you." Use the power of the bSwitch to make a bold statement (right or wrong). You will be respected for having a point of view.	"Well maybe if BOB was smarter, younger, or a better leader THEN we'd be more successful!" Too much description is never a good thing when you're trying to get something you want. In this case, you want the RESPECT of your boss. You DON'T want to talk behind his back and insult him! Do it to his face!
What do you get out of always pleasing everyone?	"I get joy out of pleasing others. But sometimes that joy dissipates when my needs are ignored." You'll never SHINE when you're busy making everyone else look good! Remember that the next time you give a coworker a compliment in front of the boss!	"The PROMOTION that I deserve, of course!" Doing nice things for others is not a bad thing. But make sure that what you want in RETURN, YOU GET! It's not being greedy—it is testing the boundary of your professional or personal relationship.	"It's not worth my while to be nice or accommodating to those around me...EVER." It CAN be worth your while to please those around you— if you MAKE it worth your while! Strive for a win-win outcome.

Question	Non-Assertive TURN IT UP!	Assertive JUST RIGHT	Aggressive TONE IT DOWN!
Surely, Violet, you don't mind helping me with this one little thing.	"No problem. I will DO it!" Don't agree to do things if you don't have time or won't be able to concentrate on doing a good job! If you're unsure of how to respond, a pause and a little SILENCE will go a long way. By thinking before you make a decision, you will force your coworker to reconsider the request.	"I will let you know." In politics you will notice that a politician never answers a question directly. He is evasive. When asked, "Can you commit to this bill or this policy?" the politician says, "I will give it my full consideration" or "Let me give that some thought and I will have someone from my staff let you know one way or another." Be strategic when you respond. Then step away for a second and consider if in fact you have the time to take on yet another thing.	"Absolutely not." By refusing right off the bat, you come across as aggressive and confrontational—not at all like the team player who is on her way to a big promotion (which is what you get if you use your bSwitch correctly and effectively)!

Question	Non-Assertive TURN IT UP!	Assertive JUST RIGHT	Aggressive TONE IT DOWN!
You're useless.	"Yeah, I guess." By offering your defeat so quickly you exhibit a complete lack of self-worth and value. If you don't believe you're the BEST, no one around you will either!	"I reject what you are saying. I know who I am and what I am worth. You don't define me! I am a winner!" Successful people understand the power of ME, that is, the power of believing that they are always RIGHT.	"You're an A*#%$*!" Being downright MEAN and INCONSIDERATE isn't going to get you any further in life. So if this is your response, turn it down or get out!

"I would call you a BITCH...if you were nicer."

W.W.O.D.

Omarosa,
Being a mom means your level of "sternness" multiplies by a thousand. But the line between "bitchy" and "stern" gets really fine, and sometimes it's hard to tell which is which—especially when you're a woman.

I recently went on a field trip with my daughter's fourth-grade class. The class was totally out of control—spitting, jumping off of concrete ledges, disappearing—and the teachers were nowhere to be found 90 percent of the time. I decided then and there to take my daughter out of that school at the end of the year…but not without writing a sternly worded letter to the school's principal, in which I named each and every one of her teachers' names. These teachers, I was later told, would not be returning to class the following year.

Was that going too far? Do you have any advice on how to make sure a "sternly worded letter" doesn't become a bitch manifesto?

–Guilty Mom, Los Angeles, CA

Dear Guilty,
I'm glad you brought this subject up. The WRITTEN BITCH is almost as important in this day and age than the SPOKEN BITCH. Bitch Switch etiquette in e-mails is much tougher, so rule #1 is to have your conversation in person, not over the Internet. If you absolutely must conduct business via e-mail, use the same standards you would face-to-face: No smiley faces, no casual language, no rambling, and no sugary closings. "Sincerely" is foolproof.

Good luck!
Omarosa

A Bitch With No Switch Is Like a Doggie With No Bite!

"You may be disappointed if you fail, but you are doomed if you don't try." -Beverly Sills

How to communicate in interpersonal relationships is vital—it's often the make-or-break factor in romance!

Let's take a very common situation that happens to every single woman. You're dating a guy you like and he calls one day and says, "Hey, what are you up to tonight?" I always respond, "Why do you ask?" If you don't have firm plans, but go on and on about all the things you have to do, like "Cleaning out my closets, and then I'm going to walk the dog and visit my mother," he'll be BORED!

When you eventually get around to asking why, he might have been planning to say something like, "Thought we'd see a movie." Some long drawn-out explanation of your busy life might make him think, "Oh, never mind—she's got so much to do." On the other hand, he might just be making idle conversation, so the answer is never, "Nothing, why?" You don't ever want to sound too eager and desperate. The correct answer is always: WHY DO YOU ASK?

W.W.O.D.

Dear Omarosa,
I'm such a big fan of yours. To the people who call you a bitch, well, they've never met me.

I know it's pretty normal for a guy's friends to hate his girlfriend. But my boyfriend just recently gave me an ultimatum: Be nice to his friends or "You're fired," as Donald Trump would say. Apparently they think I'm a bitch and it's becoming a problem.

I really don't think I should have to be cordial to the beer-guzzling assholes who've destroyed our living room, cracked our flat-screen TV, left bottles of booze all over the floor of my car and on our front lawn, and who are downright disrespectful to the female race in general. I hate to lose my boyfriend over this, but I want to stand my ground. I think being a girlfriend too often means you have to be babysitter, and I refuse to do that. Do you think I've crossed the "bitch" line?

Your advice is much appreciated and will be promptly forwarded to my boyfriend, who's coincidentally afraid of you.

Thx so much,
Michelle

Dear Michelle,
You know as well as I do that your friends are a reflection of...YOU! So perhaps your issue isn't with "the guys" but is actually with your boyfriend.

Although you've made your expectations clear to him, he clearly isn't living up to the male standard that YOU require (and he never will). Be honest with yourself—and him—and get out of there and find someone who fits you.

Good luck!
Omarosa

* * *

Omarosa,
I've heard that "men marry bitches," but that's a flat-out lie.

I'm twenty-five, looking to marry, and yet I can't keep a man for longer than a month or two! I've been told by people that I look mean, and I pride myself on being a bitch in control. I ooze confidence in the way I dress, talk, and act. So if men really do like bitches, why don't I have one?

Sincerely yours,
Single Bitch

Dear Single,
Honey, men DO love confident women. Maybe it's not you—it's the men you've found. Keep looking—I'm sure you'll find someone who can keep up with your wit and assertiveness one day…if you don't scare him away first! Hang in there.

And good luck!
Omarosa

Dealing With the Most Difficult People

"Life is the only real counselor. Wisdom unfiltered through personal experience does not become a part of the moral tissue." –Edith Wharton

Now you have all of these great communication skills—but what if you're still encountering problems? What if there are difficult people standing between you and your goals, and it seems like there's no way around them?

Remember that you can't change the difficult person but you can learn to cope with one. Here are some effective strategies to do so:

- **REMAIN CALM**
- **DON'T ACCUSE OR JUDGE**
- **DON'T ARGUE OR INTERRUPT**
- **REMEMBER THAT THEY ARE PROBABLY VENTING**
- **TRY DEFUSING, FOGGING, REFOCUSING, ASSERTIVE QUESTIONING, OR THE BROKEN RECORD METHOD**

DEFUSING. When you can sense someone's blood boiling, when you think things might get physical, you need to defuse the situation. Note: You're not solving the long-term problem, but you are offering a short-term solution to help that person's anger subside and for you not to do something you might regret. You can do it easily with words, like this:

Carol: I think it's best that we stop seeing each other for a little while.
Jimmy: ARE YOU KIDDING ME? WHAT THE HELL! YOU CAN'T LEAVE ME! I'M THE BEST THING YOU EVER HAD!
Carol: Listen, Jim, I know this is upsetting to you. Just calm down and realize this is what's best for us right now.

BROKEN RECORD. This technique is persistence, used to get your request across, even in the face of resistance. By repeating your needs, you can make sure your requests are clearly responded to. Of course, it doesn't always end the way you want, especially when dealing with an overly pushy person or one that simply does not care about YOU. Often, you have to make some kind of threat to get what you want—although nothing drastic. In this case, you might have to tell the manager that you will be taking your business elsewhere or telling your friends and family what a lousy store it is. Overall, this technique is a great tool—don't be afraid to use it!

Here's an example of how the Broken Record method would look:

Saleswoman: Hello. How can I help you today?

Regina: Hello. This skirt did not fit and I would like my money back, please.

Saleswoman: We don't do refunds. But we can give you store credit.

Regina: I am returning this skirt for a full refund; it doesn't fit, and I would like my money back.

Saleswoman: Is it too big or too small? Maybe we can find one in your correct size.

Regina: Please return this skirt. I would like my money back.

Saleswoman: Since the skirt hasn't gone on sale, I'm happy to give you store credit for the full price of the skirt.

Regina: No, I don't want credit. I want the money I paid for the skirt, please.

Saleswoman: I'm really not sure if I can do that. I'll have to get an authorization— can you wait here for a moment?

Regina: Yes.

Manager: How can I help you?

Regina: As I told your employee, I need to return this skirt—it just doesn't fit—and I would like a full refund.

Manager: There's no other size you'd like? I'm sure we could find one for you in the back if you don't see it out here.

Regina: Let me be clear—I don't want the skirt. I would like to return it and I would like my money back.

Manager: OK. I'll be able to authorize the return THIS time.

Regina: Thank you!

FOGGING. When people talk down to you or criticize you, what do you say in response? Using this method, you appear to side with the person speaking to you, although you never actually ADMIT any wrongdoing. You're not conceding—you are avoiding conflict and minimizing communication. This one can come in handy when speaking to someone who wields great power over you—for example, a boss who has the power to fire you.

Boss: This report is kind of brief. I thought you would have more to say on this subject.

Mildred: Yes, it is brief. Ever heard of "Keep It Simple, Stupid"?

Boss: Why did you cover so many subjects? I think you probably could have stuck to one.

Mildred: I will consider that for next time.

Boss: Well, it's important that you do these reports right, as the rest of the company will be using this format.
Mildred: Thanks for that feedback.

ASSERTIVE QUESTIONING. When someone has a NEGATIVE reaction to something you've said or asked, often a good way to confront the person is by responding with a question yourself. This way people are forced to evaluate what they're saying and why they are so negative—and you can get to the bottom of the issue.

Professor Belinda: Did you turn in your report today?
Carl: Why are you always picking on me? What did I do?
Professor Belinda: Why do you think this is about me picking on you?
Carl: Because I thought you were singling me out in front of everyone.

REFOCUSING. This one is exactly how it sounds. A lot of difficult people choose to change the subject—that is their way of dealing with problems. In that case, you have to step up and be the one to make sure you direct the conversation where you want it to go!

Stephanie: James, you told me you would pick me up at 5 o'clock. You were half an hour late!

James: Did you do your makeup differently?

Stephanie: We're not talking about my makeup right now. It's rude to be so late without calling.

James: Well, we'll still make the movie.

Stephanie: Yes, but do you understand that I was ready half an hour ago? I could have done a million different things in the time that I spent waiting.

James: If you want, we can just go to dinner. We can skip the movie.

Stephanie: That's not the point. Are you even listening to me?

James: Okay. I'm sorry I was late. It won't happen again.

W.W.O.D.

Omarosa,
I'm writing to you from a little town in the South where I happened to be visiting family for the weekend. We had an "episode" last night that I thought you could use.

A large party of fifteen (including myself) went into a restaurant for a celebratory dinner. A friend of mine had made reservations over three weeks ago and called twice that day to confirm. Unfortunately when we arrived at the hostess desk, the young hostess said our reservation had been "lost." After my friend explained to her that we had reservations for three weeks and had a large party of fifteen, she said it would be about ten minutes. A half an hour later I had to literally beg my friend to speak to the manager. The manager said he would take care of us. Another fifteen minutes later, we were taken to a table not in a private room (as the reservation specified) but out in the open. By the time our waitress got to the table and asked us what drinks we wanted, I said, exasperated, "We don't even have a wine list!"

Dinner turned out nicely, but needless to say I will never recommend this restaurant again.

Here's where my question comes in. After eating, my fourteen friends could not get over how I treated the waitress and claimed that I had "made a scene" the entire time we were waiting to be seated. "So what!" was my thinking.

I thought I'd let you decide: Who's right?

If you say my friends are correct, the next dinner's on me.

Sincerely,
Pushy in Palm Springs

Dear Pushy,
Dealing with difficult people is...difficult! There's no doubt about it. When people lie to you or ignore you, you have a tendency to go after them...aggressively. But being too aggressive doesn't get your point across—it often makes things worse! I think you were right in going to the manager, but went overboard taking out your frustration on the waitress (who probably had no control over what was happening at the door). You and your friends—tied for first?

Omarosa

Silence Can Be So Loud!

"If it don't make dollars,
it don't make sense."
—Ervin Bernard Reid

Once you've worked out how to communicate verbally in the most effective manner, there are ways to make an impact without even saying one word at all. Remember, upwards of 60 percent of all communication is nonverbal. We all communicate without words in so many ways, in everything from how we dress and smile to gesture and nod. We even communicate through scent. I have a bottle of unisex fragrance with a very masculine top note, and I wear that fragrance to negotiations. I want to communicate in every way that I am powerful and in charge.

Silence communicates volumes when you are in face-to-face situations, too. I've been on the receiving end of many a tirade, both on reality shows and in real life. In situations like that, silence equals power. There are times when it's best to say nothing. After people have worn themselves out yelling while you sit calmly, if you respond with silence then at some point they'll be forced to try to make you say something. They have to try to draw you out. Also, silence is a potent weapon in negotiations, and we'll elaborate more on that in the next part of this book!

Recently I had a meeting with my money manager, who was going on and on about general economic conditions and the poor general outlook. The gist of what he was telling me was that I needed to cut back. "We need to cut back here, and here, and you don't need to spend this much on that...."

I sat silently, looking at him, and waiting for him to get to the point. After a long pause, I responded. "How about if we cut back on your commission? Given the poor economic environment, wouldn't you agree that's a good place to start?"

And I continued to sit there silently while he thought that over and sputtered; I didn't qualify or temper my remarks because I'd made my point quite clearly. The meeting ended satisfactorily, with him figuring out ways for me to diversify and earn more money, which is his job, instead of the proposed extreme cutbacks. "Give up my manicures and pedicures?" I argued. Things can't be that bad!

Turning Down the Volume but Turning Up the Heat!

"A woman's dress should be like a barbed-wire fence: serving its purpose without obstructing the view."
—Sophia Loren

It goes without saying that we communicate with adornments—a watch, purse, shoes, and so on. A rainbow pin could indicate that the wearer is a supporter of the gay community. An American flag button says that someone is patriotic. A pink ribbon on the lapel could signify that the wearer supports breast cancer research. When women want to appear welcoming and non-threatening, they tend to wear their hair down. For a business meeting, they tie it back into a bun. Every person you meet offers hundreds of clues before saying a word. Learn to read them!

Gestures and mannerisms are an area where women lose much of their power. Fidgeting is a sign of weakness, and though it's very easy to do without realizing you're doing it, don't! Playing with their hair, chewing on a pen, searching in their bags for pens or business cards, blinking too much, smiling too readily, laughing inappropriately—all of these things make women appear nervous and therefore weak.

It's important to stay on the same eye level as the person in authority. If your boss is seated, you need to be seated. At no time should you be seated while someone stands over you; it immediately puts you in the lower position. One of my coworkers at the Wireless Communications Association had an abrasive personality. She used to come into the office yelling, so whenever

I heard her coming, I immediately stood up from my desk and met her face to face, looking her in the eyes while she went off on her tirade. There was no way I was going to sit meekly and have some harridan standing over me, yelling. I wanted her to feel she was dealing with an equal. I refuse to project inadequacy—and YOU SHOULD TOO!

BITCH SWITCH EXERCISE
NONVERBAL TOOLS FOR COMMUNICATING

BODY LANGUAGE DRIVES HOME YOUR MESSAGE!

Experts say we give more than 50 percent of our communication nonverbally. If your body is saying one thing while your lips are saying another, people won't be able to hear your lips.

On the next page are some common body language activities. Can you identify which would signify a positive reaction (P) and which a negative one (N)?

Smiling
Sitting forward in your chair
Frowning
Rolling your eyes
Withdrawing
Not moving
Hanging your head down or toward your shoulder
Sighing
Looking unhappy
Scowling
Shaking your head
Folding your arms across your chest
Narrowing your eyes
Drumming your fingers
Shrugging your shoulders
Swishing your foot
Bouncing your leg
Puffing your cheeks
Slumping in your chair
Staring at the person
Looking away constantly
Playing with a pencil
Nodding your head
Looking critical
Glancing at a clock
Holding a hand over your mouth

W.W.O.D.

Dear Omarosa,
I don't have a lot of money, and it's hard to survive, much less keep my wardrobe looking fresh and professional. All of the women I work with look so sharp. How can I do that on a budget? Business suits are so expensive!

Please advise,
Sharon Tell

Dear S.T.,
Like I always say: Fake it till you make it! There are plenty of resources for women who can't afford to buy a new suit every week. Because you're right—they ARE expensive! Here are some easy options that will keep you looking professional and serious about your career:

1. **Shopping at thrift stores—every now and then you'll find a designer suit that's in good condition. At the very least, look for suits in black or blue—they tend to hold up longer, look nicer, and can be accessorized with scarves, jewelry, shoes, and bags, which are also all available at your nearest thrift store.**
2. **There are programs like the Women's Alliance (in twenty-one states) and the "Dress For Success" program (which has affiliates in thirty-seven states) that make gently used professional clothing available to women.**
3. **Hand-me-downs from siblings, parents, and friends will work in a stitch. Plus, you can tell everyone your outfit is "vintage," a look that's always in style.**

Good luck!
Omarosa

Always Make an Entrance

"So if diva means giving your best, then yes, I guess I am a diva." -Patti LaBelle

Earlier in the book we discussed the role that confidence plays in developing your bSwitch. Never miss an opportunity to let your light shine! Seize the spotlight and seize the moment! It should come as no surprise that I take this to heart, and I never miss an opportunity to make an entrance! A woman can teach people how to treat her and respond to her, and it starts when she enters the room. Doormats walk into a room tentatively, headdown, like they've already been defeated. No!

Take a deep breath, turn on the bSwitch, and make your entrance. You will feel the power surge as you stand up straight and tall, put your head back, and stride confidently forward. You want your entrance to say, "I am a powerful woman, and you will treat me accordingly."

LEARN FROM THE PSYCHO SWITCH... JANICE DICKINSON, THAT IS!

The Detonator

There is a Switch who is so hazardous that, if she is not properly recognized and managed, can cause you great harm. Actually, this Switch is not a Switch at all–she is a Detonator who can, and will, explode (or implode) at any moment. I have encountered a Switch like this firsthand: Janice Dickinson, celebrity judge on Tyra Banks's *America's Next Top Model*.

In 2005, I joined the eccentric celebrity cast of *The Surreal Life,* which included Jose Canseco, Bronson Pinchot, Sandy Denton, Carey Hart, and Janice Dickinson. During the course of the show we had to complete various tasks that included: renovating a battered-women's shelter, competing in an all-star baseball game in Las Vegas, and participating in a bowling tournament designed to raise funds for developmentally challenged youth.

It was during this bowling tournament that I first saw the DETONATOR in action.

The "Surreal Lifers" were competing against the Sunshine Strikers, a team made up of teenagers who were mentally and developmentally disabled. I eventually wound up volunteering to serve as the captain of the Sunshine Strikers.

The kids on my team were fired up and ready to win. They chanted and jeered at the *Surreal Life* team in a playful manner. But Janice Dickinson took their enthusiasm personally.

Suddenly, in full view of the rest of the *Surreal Life* team and hundreds of thousands of home viewers, Janice began to lob insults at the Sunshine Strikers as if she were lobbing hand grenades. She called them every derogatory term ever used to insult the mentally challenged. She used her Detonator Switch to attack each and every one of them and did not let up throughout the tournament.

Her despicable behavior was a clear example of the type of Switch that you have to get as far away from as possible. Don't try to reason with a person like Janice. Clearly she did not care about destroying the morale of the Sunshine Strikers or losing what little integrity she'd already shown.

When you come across a woman who has a DETONATOR, remember that these individuals are hurting themselves as much as they are trying to hurt YOU. Keep your distance and avoid conflict with this type of Switch. Otherwise there could be an explosion with a casualty of one—YOU!

Bitch Switch Tips!

- Vocalize your wants and use affirmations to guide you!
- CCT: Always be CLEAR, CONCISE, and THOROUGH!
- Sometimes the best answer is: "WHY DO YOU ASK?"
- KNOW WHEN TO SHUT UP!
- Seize the spotlight, and seize the moment!

PART V

Negotiating with
THE SWITCH

"Let us never negotiate out of fear.
But let us never fear to negotiate."
–John Fitzgerald Kennedy

Bitch Switch Negotiation Rule
Number One–Ask!

*"If you can't go around it, over it,
or go through it, you had better negotiate with it."
-Ashleigh Brilliant*

People ask me all the time where I got my knack for negotiation. I usually respond, "I get it from the YO"—that is, Youngstown, Ohio, one of the most dangerous cities in America. Along with my B.A. and M.A. degrees, I have a degree from the "school of hard knocks."

Growing up in an inner-city housing project, I learned that negotiation skills meant the difference between life and death. During my years in high school, more than ten of my classmates were killed. I never liked the idea of fighting, so in order to avoid it at all costs, I became a skilled negotiator at an early age. Certainly, growing up in an area that prized toughness affected my personality. I learned very early on not to let people push me around and to never take **NO** for an answer.

Nowadays everyone I meet asks me about my encounters with the powerful men that I have worked with like Bill Clinton, Al Gore, heavyweight champion Lennox Lewis and even Gene Simmons. But the person I am asked about most is the president of the Trump

Organization, Donald J. Trump. Trump is, first and foremost, a master negotiator and dealmaker! It's not because he has a long list of extreme tactics up his sleeves. His main tactic is that he makes demands that no one else dreams of making. In the late seventies and early eighties, when no one else was offering high-end luxury living in New York City, Trump negotiated unique deals that allowed him to secure loans with little collateral, and he strategically took advantage of sizable tax breaks. His strategy was simple! He simply *asked*!

There is one little tool that will increase the likelihood of winning in dealmaking and negotiations by 1,000 percent! It's called **ASKING.** Many women don't get what they want because they don't even bother to ask!

W.W.O.D.

Omarosa,
I'm a "yes" person—I've just never been able to say no. As such,
I'm an AWFUL negotiator, especially when it comes to money!
I tend to take the first offer that comes my way, even though I
know it's not the best I can get.

Do you have any tips on how (as a woman) to be a better
negotiator?

This is something I can't afford to wait any longer to learn....

Much obliged,
Yes Ma'am

Dear Yes Ma'am,
Learning how to say NO and negotiate your happiness
can't be taught in five minutes. It's a lifestyle change, and
hopefully my book will get you in the right frame of mind.
If you think of saying NO and negotiating your worth as
a simple "turning on" and "turning off" of the bSwitch,
you'll find it's easier than you could have ever imagined!
Here are some other quick tips:
Never tell an employer what you "need"—speak only in
terms of what you're "worth" and don't hesitate to
overreach...you're worth it!
After the first offer is made (DO NOT take any job
without discussing salary beforehand) keep quiet! By not
speaking, you are nonverbally saying NO while opening
wage negotiations.
NEGOTIATE, period. Men are four times more likely to
negotiate their salary than women are, putting women at
a severe disadvantage in the workplace!

Hope these tips help. Good luck!
Omarosa

"Hell No" Is the Beginning of the Negotiation

"God gave women intuition and femininity. Used properly, the combination easily jumbles the brain of any man I've ever met." -Farrah Fawcett

In preparation for writing this book I conducted hundreds of informal interviews with women about their personal challenges. One thing became clear to me. Women are afraid to negotiate, because they are afraid of the word NO. They go to great lengths to avoid hearing or saying the word NO. In the workplace, at home, in all those small daily interactions, the word NO looms like a dark cloud. A doormat sees this word as a rejection, the end. The bSwitch allows you to see it as a CHALLENGE, the beginning of the negotiation.

I have found that most things in life worth having are worth fighting for. So there is no reason to fear being told NO. I have learned to use my bSwitch as something akin to a shield, and I use it to ensure that I get what I want. NO is not a barrier that can't be overcome and it should not be for you. You will face adversity at every single turn, so learn to anticipate it. As a skilled and competitive lifelong chess player, I have learned the importance of staying three moves ahead.

It used to be that NO was the beginning of the negotiation for me, but as the stakes have gotten higher, it's advanced into a finite "HELL, NO!" We women know all too well what it's like to keep hitting the same glass ceiling and treading on sticky floors for so long. These barriers require a change in attitude, from NO to HELL, NO!

Now You've Got the Switch. Why Not Use It?

*"Being powerful is like being a lady.
If you have to tell people you are, you aren't."*
-Margaret Thatcher

Whether we are comfortable with the process or not, at some point we are going to have to negotiate. After all, we engage in many small negotiations throughout every day of our lives. My sweet older sister, Gladys, for example, has a teenage son, Jalen, who wanted to stay out late with his friends one night until midnight, past his 10 p.m. curfew. They negotiated back and forth and finally decided upon 11 p.m. as a compromise. At work, a client wants a report turned in on Wednesday instead of the previously agreed-upon date of Friday. After some discussion, we agree that he will get the report by the end of Thursday. You see an ad in the newspaper for the perfect mattress set for your guest room. When you walk into the store, the price actually turns out to be $100 higher. What should you do? NEGOTIATE!

With the bSwitch tools outlined in this section, you will enter negotiations with confidence and be certain to come out on top—or at least not on the bottom! Using the switch can mean several things: being proactive when you need to be, taking control of a situation when called for, and lying low when necessary.

I have a close friend, Gwen, who hates the whole idea of being assertive or bringing attention to a situation, even if she's being taken advantage of. I explained to her that she can be appropriately assertive at the right moment, then go back to her passive ways once she's treated fairly, as she deserves. Gwen is not changing from the kind, sweet-natured person that she's always been—she's simply flipping on her bSwitch to get what she wants.

You don't have to be a bitch to be good at negotiations. You may, however, have to flip on your bSwitch in order to draw the necessary power to stop being pushed around by those who are accustomed to taking advantage of your kindness.

Bitch Switch Tips for Negotiating

"Difficulties mastered are opportunities won."
-Winston Churchill

Over the course of my career I've certainly engaged in my fair share of conflicts, disagreements, and catfights, some of which probably could have been avoided; others were a long time coming. In life, as in reality TV, conflict is inevitable. There will always be somebody who does not like you, how you carry yourself, or the way you conduct your business. Negotiation is the key to avoiding or managing these conflicts when they arise.

Stop being so agreeable! The whole point of negotiation is to come out with an understanding between two parties. Once an agreement has been reached, the process ends. But if you agree to everything your opponent wants at the very beginning, then you have no chance. My friend and accountant, LaVern, for example, tells her son, "I'm going to let you go to the baseball game this weekend. But only after you take out the trash."

LaVern should use the power of the bSwitch to say: "Take out the trash all week, then I'll consider taking you to the baseball game on Saturday." Don't hand things over and give up leverage before any negotiation has even taken place! You will completely undermine your position from the start.

Bitch Switch: from fear to fearless! We as women tend to be our own worst enemies when it comes to getting what we want. Because of our discomfort with the negotiation process, we will do anything to end it as quickly and painlessly as possible. This leads to making quick and unfortunate concessions. During my M.A. studies at Howard University, I worked part-time in corporate and residential leasing for Charles E. Smith Realty. I used to hear my coworker Noelle say, "I'll do it this time, but don't expect this all the time." The ONLY time that matters is THIS TIME! She constantly shifted her position lower because of a perception that to do otherwise might hurt her relationship. Don't ever lowball yourself! It undermines your success.

Be clear. Powerful negotiation starts with impactful communication. Remember what my favorite journalism professor, Dr. Emil Dansker, used to tell me? CCT: Always strive to be clear, concise, and thorough.

Listen up! Better communication leads to effective negotiation. Most women are unable to recognize that they are even in a negotiation because they haven't honed their listening skills. My publicist, Priscilla Clarke, is a master at finding opportunities simply by listening. She is able to find deals where none existed before. How does Priscilla do it? She asks herself: Is there an opportunity here? What can I leverage in this situation?

Approach negotiations boldly. When you enter a negotiation, make sure that you do so BOLDLY. Approach each and every negotiation—whether it's getting an extra shot of espresso at Starbucks or a better deal on your lawn services—with the belief that you can and will win!

Get specific. Most women fight for control, not results. Always be specific about what you want. Remember, it's not personal, it's business!

Be confident of your value. At a job interview, you might hear, "There are other candidates who will take this salary and do this job for less."

When faced with this type of idle threat, flip the switch and say:

"I am confident that my credentials and experience exceed that of those bargain-basement candidates!"

Your confidence and ability to illustrate your own value is sure to give you the upper hand—and take you out of the defensive position.

In every deal you must always remember to point out what value you are bringing to the table. The challenge then becomes how to make that value your commodity. Find the clearest, most concise way to communicate your value.

Beware the gender trap. It is important to avoid clear gender traps inherent in negotiation. When men are aggressive and downright mean (as was the case with Piers Morgan on *Celebrity Apprentice*) it is widely considered to be part of his game plan or strategy. No one ever perceived Piers as crossing the line or being outrageous! Because of underlying gender bias he was perceived as a tough businessman using tactics that come with playing in the big leagues with the big boys. When women match that level of aggressiveness, they are perceived as emotional, out of control, or crazy. Keeping your emotions in check during intense negotiations will help you get further.

Practice—so you're ready for big negotiations. When it comes to major negotiations—your salary, a prenup, a mortgage, things that you have to live with forever—then it is really time to fight. That's when you have to FLIP ON YOUR SWITCH, not say, "Oh, next time." The average car loan is for three to five years; the average mortgage is thirty years. The average marriage lasts five to eight years and the average career...a lifetime. If you don't fight for a good deal now, you will be stuck with the results of your weak negotiation skills for a long, long time.

Just say no! If you make a statement emphatically, people will respond. You must learn to say no to a bad deal or bad terms—at once, firmly, and without long explanations. There are many manipulators in the world, and no shortage of people who can't stand up for themselves. The asker, whether it is your boss or a salesperson, will quickly move on. They just want something done. If they see you're not going to do it, they are on to the next poor soul. These individuals are exploiters, and they'll move on to the next person and the next until they find someone to do what they want. Don't worry—they will! Takers only respond to one kind of communication: an emphatic NO!

The first step is learning how to recognize them, because takers have very sophisticated social skills. They know how to turn on the charm and charisma to make you do what they want. Most people who drive you crazy don't wake up in the morning thinking about how to make your life miserable. They don't stay up nights planning how to ruin your day. What they do is whatever you let them do...they will push you as far as you will be pushed. It's nothing particularly personal—but if you don't use your bSwitch, what's going to stop them? For them it's easy because there are no consequences to walking all over you. Use your Bitch Switch to end this kind of behavior.

Question Authority

"Elegance is refusal." -Coco Chanel

I have never had any fear of authority. I am respectful to people in positions of authority, but that doesn't mean that I will robotically do whatever they say because they're in charge. One of the companies that my firm represented was run by a woman who hated challenging authority. She often solicited my help to deal with such situations. If someone whom she deemed an authority figure said something was so, for her, IT WAS SO! I tried time and time again to explain to her, and I try to explain to other women like her, that you don't have to take everything at face value. It's okay to ask questions for clarification or when you are uncomfortable with what's being presented! Most of the time, what is being said is merely that person's opinion or translation of a policy.

A perfect example of such a case is hotel check-in. I travel extensively and stay at some of the best hotels across the country. My event sponsors are always asked to cover room cost, taxes, and any and all incidentals. When I check into a hotel, the clerk asks for a credit card for incidental charges, even though I know that the sponsor has faxed the appropriate authorization to cover all my hotel expenses. It never fails. For some reason, the clerks always give the same song and dance, which forces me to flip on my bSwitch.

On a recent occasion at a hotel in Times Square, a clerk refused to accommodate me because it was hotel policy to ALWAYS collect a credit card from every guest who checked in. He kept insisting that I hand over my personal credit card, even though he had the authorization from my event sponsor. After a long talk with the hotel's front desk manager, the general manager, and eventually the corporate office, it turned out that I was right. There it was, in black and white, the incidentals authorized and covered. The woman at headquarters apologized profusely and couldn't understand how the situation had escalated to her level; she thought that it could have been resolved if the person at the front desk had just listened to what I was saying.

The point of this story is that, had I not challenged the hotel clerk, I would have had to hand over my credit card, and the whole room might very well have been charged to me—mistakes like that happen all the time. They would also have my confidential information, which is what I was fighting to protect in the first place. The additional thirty minutes I spent calling and talking with various hotel employees was well worth protecting my financial privacy. As a result of my inconvenience, I negotiated an upgrade to the presidential suite and a lavish spa day, which helped me to forget the incident ever happened! I was able to secure these concessions because I refused to roll over. The clerk must have said ten times, "It's our policy." I must have said eleven times, "HELL, NO!"

See It in Writing

"Any intelligent woman who reads the marriage contract, and then goes into it, deserves all the consequences."
-Isadora Duncan

I make it a habit to always ask to see the written policies people refer to. Recently, I took my nephew to the library near Momarosa's house in L.A. to get a library card. The librarian refused to give him one, because I wasn't his official guardian. After some back and forth, I asked to see the official policy. The policy was vague and stated that in the case of a minor applying for a card, the minor had to show ID and the person accompanying him or her had to provide a driver's license or identification card. I had plenty of identification, including my nephew's learner's permit.

"Your interpretation of the policy is wrong," I told her. I couldn't believe that she was giving us a hard time. Here is a kid who actually wanted to read a book instead of play video games, and she was discouraging him due to her inaccurate interpretation of the policy. She thought "adult" meant "legal guardian," as if someone was going to walk around with official adoption papers in a wallet. It was ridiculous. We left with the library card, of course—it was hard enough to drag my nephew away from his PlayStation in the first place! We weren't about to leave without his library card, and simple, straightforward negotiation of the written policy did the trick!

Don't Be Afraid of Contracts!

Krystle Carrington: You're trying to buy me off!
Alexis Carrington: People buy and people sell and
I am a master at both! –"Dynasty"

Contracts are to be negotiated! Too many people, especially women, get intimidated by legalese. For example, when I was on the show *Fear Factor*, part of the contract stipulated that I "might" be responsible for the car used in one of the stunts. That's ridiculous— this was *Fear Factor*, where things get blown up and crashed every episode! Contracts are to be read and revised. If you have questions, ask them until you get the clarification that you need to make an informed decision. And negotiate, negotiate, negotiate!

When moved into my New York City pied-à-terre, the management office informed me that I was only allowed to use one local provider for cable and Internet. Well, last time I checked, we live in the the U.S. of A, and America is all about choices, so I asked to see the contract that the building made on behalf of its tenants with this cable company. It turned out that I could get satellite service from any company I chose, that the building only had cable rights. So I found a better package from a satellite provider instead of paying twice as much as everybody else in the building for less! Of course, the building gets kickbacks from everybody who signs up, but I got the best deal because I asked to see the contract.

I am constantly open to learning all I can about every situation. It's like being a detective—staying in the information-gathering mode. Information is power—gather as much information as you can, so you can formulate the most effective negotiation strategies.

Fair is Fair

When I was on the set of the VH1 hit show *The Surreal Life*, I noticed that baseball slugger Jose Canseco was meeting with his manager all the time, in spite of the fact that we as a cast were absolutely forbidden to have any visitors for the duration of the shoot. I approached the producers and demanded that they allow my mother to visit on the grounds that others were being granted this concession, so why wasn't I? They knew that they had to treat all the cast members fairly and equally, so they eventually allowed Momarosa to visit. After all, fair is fair.

The Hillary Switch

Hillary Clinton shattered so many barriers; she's gone further than any other woman in the American presidential election process, yet she was demonized by the press, which called her every name in the book while skirting around the word "bitch." Hillary had done nothing more or less than all the men in politics playing the game they'd played for 200 years, but the language they used to describe her? Dreadful. She was endlessly attacked during the election for actions that were business-as-usual for her opponents. The double standard is alive and well.

The Economist, a very sober publication, printed such a scathing commentary about her that I couldn't believe what I was reading. I mused to myself, *Maybe she should have just turned on her Bitch Switch full-throttle, gone out there and waged war.* Instead, she apologized for being too tough. She shifted in a way that I don't believe women should ever shift.

What does this have to do with NO? Well, the establishment basically told Hillary Clinton, "HELL, NO! We don't like this behavior from a woman." I wish she had said back, 'HELL, NO!' is where this battle begins!"

W.W.O.D.

Omarosa,
Have you ever thought of running for president? It's about
time this country got a good, tough bitch at the helm.

Your thoughts?

Dangling Chad

Dear Chad,
There is a saying in politics: Is it better to be a KING
or a KING-MAKER? I prefer being a KING-MAKER,
because that's where all the POWER lies.

Sincerely,
Omarosa

ALWAYS Negotiate Your Salary

"Money talks, they say. All it ever said to me was 'Good-bye.'" -Cary Grant

One of the areas that has a dramatic affect on a woman's morale in the workplace is her ineffective salary negotiations. When I polled women for this book on the topic of salary negotiation, most admitted that they never attempted to negotiate their salary fearing that they could jeopardize their new position and their reputation. It was clearly causing a great deal of anxiety and consternation. Understanding that it's not just the candidates who are uncomfortable, many of female the managers that I polled for the book admitted that they found discussing salaries with potential candidates extremely difficult! The female managers struggled with turning away a highly qualified applicant versus pushing the limits of company budget constraints.

It is important to recognize that it is YOUR responsibility as a candidate to make sure that you engage in an initial discussion about salary; do this during the first stages of the hiring process. Activate your bSwitch before you even walk though the door by doing some investigative work to determine comparable salaries for positions in similar companies. There are many resources that give information about average pay, although the best place to turn is the person who held that position previously. Be sure to give consideration to the amounts that will be extracted from your salary such as health benefits, 401K deductions, and dreaded taxes to come up with a realistic salary, expectation. **Don't LIMIT your salary expectations out of fear or reluctance to use your bSwitch.** Trust me, there is always room for salary negotiation.

Negotiate Your Happiness

"If you want the rainbow, you've got to put up with the rain." -Dolly Parton

Proper use of the bSwitch allows you to identify unreasonable demands and learn not to settle for too little or give way too much! If you are afraid of facing your customers, clients, or family because you're not strong enough, throw the bSwitch on relatives, coworkers, and staff who are constantly taking advantage. Show them that you know how to negotiate your own happiness.

The principles of the bSwitch allow you to be realistic, flexible, and tough. Becoming fearless about any negotiation allows you to develop winning strategies and tactics, no matter who your opponent might be! These skills allow you to focus on your strengths and eliminate your weaknesses. Effective negotiation is critical to your happiness and accomplishing your goals in life. Effective negotiation means that you can be confident that you have always secured the best possible result...which will help you lead a happy and productive life.

Bitch Switch Tips!

- Ask, Ask, Ask!
- HELL, NO is the beginning of the negotiation!
- Use the switch to be proactive, take control, or lie low!
- Don't hand anything over—don't give up without a fight!
- Believe in YES—you CAN and WILL get what you want!
- Sometimes you have to JUST SAY NO!
- It's not personal, it's business!

PART VI

Viva La
BITCH!

"Good girls go to heaven.
Bad girls go everywhere!"

–Omarosa

Some Cautionary Words!

"Opportunity knocked. My doorman threw him out."
–Adrienne Gusoff

Hopefully, you've now found your own bSwitch and learned how to turn it on, up, and off. But there are definite consequences for misusing your newfound power. Let's consider the following:

RESENTMENT! Of all the possible negative emotions, nothing bubbles away, festers inside, and upsets peace of mind like resentment. Once you have triggered that feeling inside somebody on the receiving end of your newfound power, there are no limits to what someone nursing resentment will do. Those people will wait weeks, months, a year nursing their resentments all the while, just waiting for a chance to get you back—or watch you fail. The best way to avoid causing resentment is by always being firm and clear about what you are trying to accomplish and by always watching your back.

When you are trying to accomplish an objective, you have to learn to manage your leadership style so you will get the desired results without causing resentment to flare up all around you. You don't have to like the people you work with, they don't have to like you, and you don't have to sit around in a circle singing

Kumbaya, but it's critical to find a way to both motivate and encourage cooperation without causing resentment. **Get people to want what you want, not to plot your demise!** If you are surrounded by people who resent you, your objectives are doomed.

I am wiser now, much more accomplished, and have survived in both the shark-infested world of corporate America and the dog-eat-dog world of politics. In spite of all that I have been through, I am still ready to set the world on fire. Now that I'm more mature, I know that there's no reason to keep the bSwitch on full-blast in every situation.

Admitting your faults isn't an easy feat, but to progress, it's necessary. This is one of the lessons I wish I would have learned back then. Early on in my career, I made plenty of mistakes that could have been prevented by more savvy use of the switch. All I knew back then was to keep my bSwsitch on, full-throttle, all the time. Turns out, having known what would have happened as a result of my misusing the switch might have gotten me where I am faster. So without further ado, here's what NOT to do:

• *Fault-finding.* Pointing out every little thing that is wrong, instead of looking for some part of the work to praise and effectively redirecting the problem areas.

- ***Pointing fingers.*** Saying to an underling, "You didn't complete that project, did you?" instead of asking, "How's that project coming along?" is a surefire way to demotivate instead of motivate a person to do what you want.

- ***Tone.*** I am the first to admit that at times I can be condescending and abrasive. I have an edge, which I realize is just a part of my unique makeup. I encourage you to watch your "tone" when addressing others, because it can be a very strong way to either motivate or demotivate whoever you're dealing with.

- ***Temper.*** There is a difference between raising your voice and losing your temper and blowing up all the time. The bSwitch is ideally a regulator—it does not give you free rein to be a volatile, unpredictable, tantrum-throwing nightmare.

- ***Berating.*** Saying, "You are dumber than a box of rocks!" to someone when you've been driven to the absolute end of your patience may make you feel better for three seconds but will likely harm your efforts to get what you want in the long run. They will be demoralized and nothing will get accomplished. A woman in control of her bSwitch has no need to berate anybody.

• ***Destroying dignity.*** You may be working for a boss whose sole mission in life appears to be destroying your dignity and self-confidence, who attempts to undermine not only your abilities but the very essence of who you are. Now that you're armed with the bSwitch and have a strong sense of who you are, you won't be easily deterred by the remarks of a psychotic, egomaniac bitch boss. This is a cheap way she gains power.

I do realize that this may sound odd coming from a woman who was named the top television villain of all time by *TV Guide.* I'm not saying I'm perfect! Taking matters to a personal level on a reality show and trying to shred somebody's dignity in real life are two separate things. Attempting to destroy someone's dignity is the ultimate misuse of the bSwitch.

• ***Check your ego.*** In 2005 I engaged in a tense interview with Dr. Phil. On his show, I was baited by his bullying tactics and let my ego take over. Although I felt totally justified in my behavior given the circumstances, I do realize that there was a better way that I could have handled Dr. Phil that may have allowed his audience to better see my point of view.

W.W.O.D.

Omarosa,
My girlfriend is an actress—professionally, I mean. But I'm
always amazed how DRAMATIC she is even in the simplest,
most banal situations. Take today, for instance. After placing our
orders at a popular sandwich chain store, we walked up to the
register to pay. When the woman at the counter told us how much
our order cost, my girlfriend launched into an impression of the
sandwich store's commercials. I watched as the counter girl's eyes
widened in fear: "Is this crazy girl going to get me fired? What did
I do? What is she talking about?" As usual, I tried to calm the
poor worker down, explaining that my girlfriend was an actress
and was just trying to make a joke.

This kind of thing happens ON A REGULAR BASIS.

Am I wrong to be annoyed? Or should I be happy my girlfriend
is so confident with herself and her talent?

Sincerely,
Acting Up

Dear Acting Up,
Sounds like either A) your girlfriend has a serious split
personality and is unaware of her problem or B) she needs
to turn her bSwitch down a notch or two. Being
dramatically inclined myself, I can relate to your
girlfriend. But the trick is knowing when and where to use
that drama to her (and your) advantage. If she never seems
to turn her switch off, that's going to create problems for
you both. Give her a copy of my book. There is a whole
section about my days on the stage that may help her out.

Good luck!
Omarosa

* * *

Hi, O (Can I call you O?),

I'm really tired of "bitchiness" being attributed to PMS. I control my inner bitch, not my biology. What's your opinion on the matter?

Concerned,
Bloated Bea

Dear Bea,

Don't blame PMS for your problems. It sounds like you are a BITCH BY NATURE. Being a woman gets tough sometimes, but you can't let it bring you down. I thank God I'm a woman every day—think of all the great things it's afforded me. And remember: you are in control of your switch—not your boss, not your boyfriend, not PMS!

Omarosa

* * *

Dear Omarosa,
I did it! I finally made it to the top of my field. I'm happily married with a loving family—I couldn't ask for anything more. But for some reason I'm feeling unfulfilled. I tried taking up new hobbies, spending more time with my family, working out…but nothing seems to work. So what am I missing?

If you have any ideas, I'd really appreciate them.

Thanks,
Missing Something, NYC

Dear Missy,

It's not that you're missing anything—it sounds like you've got it all—but maybe it's time for you to share your success with the rest of your community. There are countless charities that you could donate your time or money to, either local, national, or global— you'll find a list of them in the back of this book. Do you feel especially indebted to a female mentor who helped you along the way? Then try becoming a mentor yourself. Do you have an abundance of work supplies or clothing that you no longer need? Give them back to a local shelter or program. One of the best perks of my Apprentice fame has been giving lectures to women all over the country. It's a true blessing to be able to share my life experiences and lessons learned with the women of America. No matter how "successful" I might feel, it's the giving that makes it all worth it. Try it and watch your emptiness magically vanish—then all you'll be missing is...nothing!

Good luck!
Omarosa

Some Final Thoughts on the BITCH SWITCH and You

"I love to see a young girl go out and grab the world by the lapels. Life's a bitch. You've got to go out and kick ass." -Maya Angelou

When I started work on this book I struggled with identifying myself so much with the word *bitch,* because I truly believe I am not one. I have an active Bitch Switch that has served me well in life. But no matter how hard I have tried to convince people how many sides there are to my personality—the funny side, the good friend, the devoted daughter, the cuddly and lovable side, and yes, the harridan-on-heels side— most will never believe it. Simply put, my name is synonymous with the word BITCH and probably always will be. "Pulling an Omarosa" is now a real pop-culture term!

I was also uncomfortable with perpetuating the use of the word *bitch,* because the academic side of me said when used incorrectly it's a derogatory, demeaning, and debilitating word. The practical side of me won out; I've realized that the word *bitch* isn't going away anytime soon. The word and all it implies is here to stay. In fact, I will openly admit to profiting from this "bitch niche" I have carved out for myself. And this book will join a long list of books that also explore this phenomenon. So why did I feel so compelled to write *The Bitch Switch*?

As you've noticed on TV and throughout this book, what I have is a highly developed power to turn my Bitch Switch on and off. The truth is, every woman has one, although there are plenty who never once turn it on. These women go through life acting like doormats, being walked all over by their bosses, families, and spouses. At the opposite extreme are the women who never turn their bSwitch off—e.g., Naomi Campbell. It's so *ON* that it could shut down all of California Power and Electric! But some women have found the perfect balance of power, like Nely Galán, Priscilla Clarke, Julie Chrystyn, and my mom, Theresa Manigault. They have mastered the art of using the bSwitch and can easily turn it up or down depending on the situation, using just the right degree of assertiveness to their advantage.

If I'm going to be known forevermore as the incarnation of the über-bitch, at least I know I've opened a dialogue on what it is that word really means and how it applies to women in general. As you've read in my book, I do a lot of lecturing on college campuses, and I have received many admiring e-mails from young women saying, "I wish I could be more assertive like you." In *The Bitch Switch*, my goal was helping them learn how to embrace their power, control it, and use it as a force for positive change in their lives. I can rest easy knowing I've helped even one woman learn how to flip on her bSwitch so she can negotiate her own happiness and ignite her life!

The reality of the modern world is that there comes a point where almost every woman is going to hear the word *bitch* applied to her—whether she is called a weak bitch, a fake bitch, a crazy bitch, or a rich bitch. That's because when people don't know how to respond to a woman, they immediately label her. The problem arises when these newly labeled women become paralyzed by the word.

Hopefully after reading this book, women all over the world will learn that there is nothing to fear from turning on the bSwitch! There is power in the bSwitch, rooted in action and energy that can transform your life. True liberation lies in freeing yourself from labels and not worrying about what people think of you. In the time you spend worrying about what other people think of you, you could be using valuable energy to focus on the things that you want and empowering yourself to go get them!

As I've said time and time again, it's almost impossible to change your entire personality and the behaviors that have been ingrained over a lifetime, and I'm not advocating that. Some women will always be naturally stronger and more assertive than others, and I know I'll never turn a shy, mousy girl into a "bitch" no matter what I write or say to her. No book can change someone's DNA. However, when you take baby steps and incorporate some of the advice contained in this book into your life, when you break the bad habits that haven't served you well and learn how to turn on your bSwitch, your life will change for the better—you'll see!

Bottom line: When a woman becomes strong, opinionated, and in charge of her own life, she automatically gets stamped BITCH. I say, "That's MISS Bitch to you!"

Signed,
The Bitch Whisperer,
Omarosa

Bitch Switch FINAL Tips!

- USE, don't ABUSE, the switch!
- SHARE your success with your community—give back!
- Don't fear the switch—embrace it!
- Flip it on and IGNITE YOUR LIFE!
- Empower YOURSELF!

For more Bitch Switch tips and updates,
visit www.OMAROSA.com

ACKNOWLEDGMENTS

To Julie Chrystyn, my "SHE-RO," and Dwight Opperman, my HERO. Thank you for never giving up on me or this project. To Michael Viner, who is a brilliant chess player on the board and in life—thank you! To Julie McCarron, Henrietta, Alina, Sal, Frank, Stephan, and the entire Phoenix Books team—thank you! A special thanks to David Kennerly for the cover photo and Vis Vitae for the post.

To my agent, Tracy Christian, and the Don Buchwald and Associates family.

To Keenan Towns and the Brand 7 Marketing Team.

To Priscilla Clarke, my angel and my publicist.

To Brian Gross, BSG PR.

To Keith Fleer and my legal team at Loeb & Loeb.

To my personal attorney, John "The Professor" Mercer!

To my Circle of Influence:

First, to my mother, Theresa Manigault, and my grandmothers, Gladys Manigault and Betty Walker. You are such amazing women who have inspired me in ways that I can't capture in words. To my sister, Gladys "Dimples" Manigault, and my brothers, Jack and Lester. To my niece and nephews, who I know will do big things in the future. To my aunties, Olivia, Brenda, Evelyn, Loretta, and Carol, and in memory of my auntie Mary Jane Walker, who passed away. To Auntie Jane and Evelyn F. and Dionne. Thank you for setting examples of how a lady should carry herself. My uncles Robert, Marvin, and Carl, for your faith, speed, and humor. To my sixty-five first cousins. I can't list you all, so I will just say I LOVE YOU CUDDIES!

To my pastor, Rev. Albert Ross Sr., and my New Grace Missionary Baptist family in Ohio. To Dr. H. Beecher Hicks and my Metropolitan Baptist Church family in D.C., who taught me to be patient, because God is not through with me yet.

To my Central State University dads: Dr. Emil Dansker, Don Anthony, and Dr. John Turk Logan. To my CSU family: Shannon R. Taylor, Brenda Stone Browder, and Vicky Whitfield and Damola Togun. For God! For Central! For State!

To my Howard University family: Dr. Gwen Bethea, Betty Goodwin, Dr. Taylor, Dr. Richard Wright, Dr. Storosta, Dr. Han, Dr. Grace Virtue, Gary Hunter, and Dr. Carol Stroman.

To my business partners: Kevin L. Jefferson, Ervin Bernard Reid, and Steve Ogunro.

To my *Apprentice* family: Donald J. Trump, Donald Jr., Ivanna, Rona, all the folks at the Trump Org, MBP, and NBC. A special thanks to Jim Dowd, Sean Martin, Amanda Ruisi, and Lee Straus.

To Nely Galán—without your powerful networking skills, kindness, and dedication, this book would not have happened.

To Marilu Henner, Nadia Comaneci, Lennox Lewis, Carey Hart, Katrina Campins, Dr. Randal Pinkett, and Trace Adkins for your continued support.

To my pageant family, Althea Smith, and all of my fellow Queeeeeens.

To my BFFs: Michael Todd and Andrew Coppa, Jeff Johnson, Astrid Tasong, Kim Bassett, Kim and Kyle Whitley, Lewis Paul Long, Michael East, Tony Powell, Norwood Young, Malesa McGee, Wendy Welch, Esdra Lamy, Michael Politz, Lushara Carter, Jocelyn Dabney, Henrietta Williams, and Wendall James.

To Michele Bohbot and Lisa Driver at Bisou Bisou, the team at Jovani, Dr. Niccole, Dr. Afifi and the entire CosmetiCare Family, Mary Glen and DeeDee Kelly (makeup artist for the book cover), and Tencia Salinas (hair for cover) at Headlines Studio.

To the thousands of students from across the country who have come to hear my lectures and the students whom I taught over the years at George Mason University, Howard University, and especially Stephan Gunther and my Communications Skills for Women students at the Graduate School, USDA. Thank you especially!

APPENDIX

BONUS
materials

SUGGESTED READING

5 Leadership Essentials for Women: Developing Your Ability to Make Things Happen by Linda Clark

The 7 Habits of Highly Effective People by Stephen R. Covey

Blink: The Power of Thinking Without Thinking by Malcolm Gladwell

The Girl's Guide to Being a Boss (Without Being a Bitch): Valuable Lessons, Smart Suggestions, and True Stories for Succeeding as the Chick-in-Charge by Caitlin Friedman and Kimberly Yorio

Gutsy Girls: Young Women Who Dare by Tina Schwager, Michele Schuerger, and Elizabeth Verdick

How to Say It For Women: Communicating with Confidence and Power Using the Language of Success by Phyllis Mindell

How to Win Friends & Influence People by Dale Carnegie

Know Yourself: A Woman's Guide to Wholeness, Radiance & Supreme Confidence by Barbara Rose

Letting Go of Your Bananas: How to Become More Successful by Getting Rid of Everything Rotten in Your Life by Daniel T. Drubin

Live Your Best Life: A Treasury of Wisdom, Wit, Advice, Interviews, and Inspiration from O, The Oprah Magazine

Nice Girls Don't Get the Corner Office: 101 Unconscious Mistakes Women Make That Sabotage Their Careers by Lois P. Frankel

The Power of Now: A Guide to Spiritual Enlightenment by Eckhart Tolle

The Purpose-Driven Life: What on Earth Am I Here For? by Rick Warren

The Quotable Bitch: Women Who Tell It Like It Really Is by Shiers C. Jessie

Self-Esteem: A Proven Program of Cognitive Techniques for Assessing, Improving, and Maintaining Your Self-Esteem by Matthew McKay and Patrick Fanning

Sisterhood of Faith: 365 Life-Changing Stories about Women Who Made a Difference by Shirley Brosius

That's Queen Bitch to You by Ed Polish and Darren Wotz

Trump: The Art of the Deal by Donald J. Trump and Tony Schwartz

Trump: Think Like a Billionaire: Everything You Need to Know About Success, Real Estate, and Life by Donald J. Trump and Meredith McIver

Why Good Girls Don't Get Ahead... But Gutsy Girls Do: Nine Secrets Every Working Woman Must Know by Kate White

Women & Money: Owning the Power to Control Your Destiny by Suze Orman

Women Don't Ask: The High Cost of Avoiding Negotiation—and Positive Strategies for Change by Linda Babcock and Sara Laschever

The Women's Book of Empowerment by Charlene M. Proctor, PhD

You Say I'm a Bitch Like It's a Bad Thing by Ed Polish and Darren Wotz

NATIONAL CHARITIES

After you've become a huge success, don't forget to share your newfound POWER with those in need around you! Here is a list of charities I endorse, followed by a long list of national charities. Surely you'll find something that piques your interest!

Omarosa's Official Charity in Compton, California
(Featured on *Celebrity Apprentice*)
www.TAMuseum.org

New Image Emergency Shelter for the Homeless
www.newimageshelter.org

Fred Jordan Mission
www.fjm.org

Jenesse Center for Domestic Violence
www.jenesse.org

Haiti Support Project
www.stateoftheblackworld.org/payonline/form2.htm

The Metropolitan Baptist Church
www.metropolitanbaptist.org

Ashoka, Innovators for the Public
www.ashoka.org

Boston Women's Health Book Collective, Inc.,
Women's Health Education/Advocacy/Consulting
www.ourbodiesourselves.org

Catalyst Inc., Expanding Opportunities for Women
and Business
www.catalyst.org

Dress for Success, Provides Interview Suits,
Confidence Boosts, and Career Development to
Low-Income Women
www.dressforsuccess.org

FINCA International, Providing Financial
Services to the World's Poorest Families
www.villagebanking.org

Global Exchange, International Human Rights
Organization
www.globalexchange.org

Global Fund for Women, Giving Grants to
Women's Groups Around the World
www.globalfundforwomen.org

Housing Assistance Council, Providing Housing
for the Rural Poor
www.ruralhome.org

Habitat for Humanity International, Building
Housing for Those in Need of Shelter
www.habitat.org

League of Women Voters, Recruiting and
Informing the Female Vote
www.lwv.org

National Council of Jewish Women, "A Faith in
the Future. A Belief in Action."
www.ncjw.org

National Council of Negro Women, Inc., Leading,
Developing, and Advocating for Women of African
Descent
www.ncnw.org

National Alliance for Caregiving, Increasing
Public Awareness of Facing Family and
Caregivers Issues
www.caregiving.org

National Congress for Community Economic
Development, a National Trade Association for
Community-Based Development Corps.
www.ncced.org

National Partnership for Women and Families,
Using Public Education and Advocacy to Help
Women and Men Meet the Dual Demands of Work
and Family
www.nationalpartnership.org

Oprah's Angel Network, Inspiring People to Make
a Difference
www.oprahsangelnetwork.org

TechnoServe, Helping Rural Men and Women
Develop Businesses for the Betterment of Their
Communities and Countries
www.technoserve.org

The National Organization for Women, Informing
and Educating the Public About Women's Rights
and Issues
www.now.org

Wider Opportunities for Women, Helping to
Achieve Economic Independence and Equality of
Opportunity for Women and Girls
www.wowonline.org

Women's Law Project, Providing Litigation,
Advocacy, Education, and Public Policy for Women
and Their Families
www.womenslawproject.org

Feminist Majority Foundation
www.feminist.org

Madre, the International Women's Human Rights
Organization
www.madre.org

National Coalition Against Domestic Violence,
NCADV
www.ncadv.org

The Princess Project, Providing Prom
Dresses/Evening Gowns to Low-Income Girls
www.princessproject.org

WEB SITES OF INTEREST

www.OMAROSA.com

www.Howard.edu

www.CentralState.edu

www.MomarosaGallery.com

www.APBSpeakers.com

www.WhiteHouse.gov

www.EWGA.com

www.visvitae.com

5 MORE PERSONALITY/ CAREER TESTS

The Keirsey Temperament Sorter
www.keirsey.com
This test will help you discover which of four types you are, leading to better insight as to which career path is right for you.

The Enneagram Institute Riso-Hudson Enneagram Type Indicator (RHETI)
www.enneagraminstitute.com
This personality test groups you into one of nine different types.

ColorQuiz
www.colorquiz.com
Based on the work of Dr. Max Luscher, this test will only take a moment, and it uses your inclination toward certain colors to give you a personality reading.

IQ Test
www.iqtest.com
To learn more about your intelligence quotient and the test, visit the above Web site.

Myers-Briggs Type Indicator (MBTI)
Grouping people into types according to the theories of Carl Jung, this is one of the most common personality assessments and can be found on the Internet.

EVEN MORE INFO ON WORKPLACE BULLYING

Excerpted from the survey performed by the Workplace Bullying Institute (WBI), bullyinginstitute.org, Copyright 2007

Zogby International conducted 7,740 online interviews of a panel that is representative of the adult population of the U.S. This is the largest national scientific survey of the phenomenon in the U.S. to date. WBI wrote the survey.

Key Findings

Workplace Bullying Is an Epidemic

37% of American workers, an estimated 54 million people, have been bullied at work. It affects half (49%) of American workers, 71.5 million workers, when witnesses are included.

Bullying Is Same-Gender/Same-Race Harassment Ignored by Current Laws

Bullying is 4 times more prevalent than illegal forms of "harassment."

American Employers Can and Do Ignore Bullying

In 62% of the cases, when made aware of bullying, employers worsen the problem or simply do nothing, despite losing an estimated 21–28 million workers because of bullying.

There Oughta Be a Law

The Workplace Bullying Institute Legislative Campaign at workplacebullyinglaw.org is attempting to effect anti-bullying state laws. 13 states have introduced the WBI Healthy Workplace Bill since 2003.

Most Bullies Are Bosses—the Stereotype Is Real

72% of bullies are bosses. 55% of those bullied are rank-and-file workers.

Bullying Most Strongly Affects Women

Women are targeted by bullies more frequently (in 57% of cases), especially by other women (in 71% of cases).

Bullying Is a Public Health Hazard

For 45% of bullied targets, stress affects their health. 33% suffer for more than one year.

Bullied Individuals Are Not "Sue Crazy"; Many Fail to Even Complain

Only 3% of bullied targets file lawsuits. 40% never complain.

Perpetrators Suffer Little Despite Inflicting Suffering

Targets have to stop the vast majority of bullying (77%) by losing their jobs, despite being the ones harmed.

BITCH SWITCH DAILY AFFIRMATIONS

1. Who cares what people think of me! I don't need their trifling validation!

2. I am not a doormat!

3. I refuse to let others define who I am!

4. I will sometimes have to yell to be heard!

5. Nagging is good and shows persistence!

6. Sometimes I'm a bitch...and I'm proud of it!

7. I will not whine, apologize, or let anything hold me back!

8. I can't make everyone like me, but I can make them respect me!

9. Remember: Hard work pays off!

10. I will recognizethat I am a woman and that makes me uniquely qualified to bitch!

THE AWAKENING

There comes a time in your life when you finally get it.... When in the midst of all your fears and insanity you stop dead in your tracks and somewhere the voice inside your head cries out: ENOUGH! Enough fighting and crying or struggling to hold on. You become like a child quieting down after a blind tantrum. Your sobs begin to subside, you shudder once or twice, you blink back your tears, and through a mantle of wet lashes you begin to look at the world through new eyes. This is your awakening.

You realize that it is time to stop hoping and waiting for something to change, or for happiness, safety, and security to come galloping over the horizon. You come to terms with the fact that he is not Prince Charming and you are not Cinderella, and in the real world there aren't always fairy-tale endings (or beginnings for that matter).

In the process, a sense of serenity is born of acceptance. You awaken to the fact that you are not perfect, and that not everyone will always love you or like you or appreciate or approve of who and what you are. And that's okay—they are entitled to their own views and opinions. You learn the importance of loving and championing yourself. You take a long look at yourself in the mirror and make a solemn promise to give yourself the same unconditional love and support you give so freely to others. In the process, a sense of newly found confidence is born of self-approval.

You stop bitching and blaming other people for the things that they did to you or didn't do for you, and you learn that the only thing you can count on is the unexpected. You learn that not everyone will always be there for you. And it is not always about you. So you learn to stand on your own and take care of yourself, and in the process a sense of safety and security is born of self-reliance. You stop judging and pointing fingers and begin to accept people as they are; to overlook their shortcomings and human frailties. In the process, a sense of peace and contentment is born of forgiveness.

You realize that much of the way you view yourself and the world around you is a result of all the messages and opinions that have been ingrained into your psyche. You will begin to sift through all the crap you've been fed about how you should behave, how you should look, how much you should weigh, what you should wear, what you should drive, how and where you shop, where you should live, what you should do for a living, who you should sleep with, who you should marry, what you should expect of marriage, the importance of having and raising children, or what you owe your kids. You learn to open up to new worlds and different points of view and begin reassessing and redefining who you are and what you really stand for.

You begin to discard the doctrines and values you've outgrown or should never have bought into in the beginning, and in the process you learn to go with your own instincts. You learn to distinguish between guilt and responsibility and the importance of setting boundaries and learning to say NO. You learn that you don't know all the answers, it's not your job to save the world, and that sometimes you just need to let go. You learn that the only cross to bear is the one you choose to carry and that martyrs get burned at the stake.

Then you learn about love. Romantic love and familial love: how to love, how much to give in love, when to stop giving, and when to walk away. You learn not to project your needs and insecurities onto a relationship. You learn that you will not be more beautiful or intelligent or lovable or important because of the man or woman you are with or the child who bears your name. You learn to look at relationships as they really are, not as you would have them be. You learn that the only love worth giving and receiving is the love that is given freely without conditions or limitations, so you stop trying to control people, situations, and outcomes. You learn that just as people grow and change, so it is with love. And you learn that you don't have the right to demand love on your own terms just to make you happy. You allow only the hands of a lover who cherishes you to glorify you with his or her touch. In the process you internalize the meaning of self-respect.

You learn that alone is not lonely; you look at the mirror and come to terms with the fact that you will never be a size five or a perfect ten, and you stop trying to compete with the image inside your head and agonizing over how you stack up. You stop working so hard at putting feelings aside, smoothing things over, and ignoring your own needs. You learn that feelings of entitlement are perfectly okay, and that it is your right to want things that you want and sometimes it's necessary to make demands. You come to realize that you deserve to be treated with love, kindness, sensitivity, and respect, and that you will not settle for less than that.

You learn to avoid toxic people and conversations. And you stop wasting time and energy rehashing your situation with family and friends. You learn that talk doesn't change things and that unrequited wishes can only serve to keep you trapped in the past. So you stop lamenting over what could or should have been and you make a decision to leave the past behind. Then you begin to invest your time and energy to effect positive change. You take a personal inventory of all your strengths and weaknesses and the areas you need to improve to move ahead. You set your goals and map out a plan of action to see things through.

You learn that your body is really your temple and begin eating a balanced diet, drinking more water, and taking more time to exercise. You learn that fatigue diminishes the spirit and can create doubts and fears, so you take more time to rest. Just as food is fuel for the body, laughter is fuel for our souls, so you take more time to laugh and play. You learn that in life, for the most part, you get what you believe you deserve, and that most of life is a self-fulfilling prophecy.

You learn that anything worth achieving is worth working for. And that wishing for something to happen is different from working toward actually making it happen. More importantly, you learn that in order to achieve success, you need direction. You need discipline. You need perseverance. You learn that nobody can do it alone, and it's okay to risk asking for help. You learn about money...the personal power and independence it brings and the options it creates. And you recognize the necessity to create your own personal wealth.

That means you learn to stop maneuvering through life merely as a *consumer* hungry for your next fix, a new dress, another pair of shoes, or looks of approval and admiration from family, friends, or even strangers who pass by. Then you discover that it is truly in giving that we receive and that the joy and abundance you seek grows out of the giving. And you recognize the importance of *creating* and *contributing* rather than *obtaining* and *accumulating*.

You learn that the only thing you must truly fear is the great robber of time: fear itself. You learn to step right into and through your fears, because you know that whatever happens you can handle, and to give into fear is giving away the right to live life on your own terms. You realize that you are in a fight for your life, and should not squander it living it under a cloud of impending doom.

You learn that life isn't always fair, you don't always get what you think you deserve, and that sometimes bad things happen to unsuspecting good people. On these occasions you learn that personalizing things is not a good idea, and that God isn't punishing you or failing to answer your prayers. It's just life happening. You learn to deal with evil in its most primal state, the id. You learn that negative feelings such as anger, envy, and resentment must be redirected or they will suffocate the life out of you and poison the universe around you.

You learn to admit when you were wrong and build bridges instead of walls. You learn to be thankful and take comfort in many of the simple things we take for granted, things that millions of people on this earth can only dream about: a full refrigerator, a full stomach, clean running water, a soft warm bed, a long hot shower. Slowly you learn to take responsibility for yourself, by yourself, and you make yourself a promise never to betray yourself and never, ever settle for less than your heart desires.

You hang a wind chime out by the window so you can listen to the wind. You make it a point to keep smiling, keep trusting, and stay open to every wonderful possibility. Finally, with courage in your heart and God by your side, you take a stand. You take a deep breath and begin to design the life you want to live as best you can.